THE BLUEBIRD YEARS

Donald Campbell and
The Pursuit of Speed

Arthur Knowles

With additional material by Graham Beech

Published by Sigma Leisure – an imprint of Sigma Press, 1 South Oak Lane, Wilmslow, Cheshire SK9 6AR, England.

British Library Cataloguing in Publication Data
A CIP record for this book is available from the British Library.

ISBN: 1-85058-766-3

Typesetting, design and project management: Sigma Press, Wilmslow, Cheshire.

Cover Design: Belvoir Cartographics & Design

Illustrations: Gelder Design & Mapping

Cover images: main picture, "The Final Curtain" – John Pittaway *(kindly provided by "Moving Images")*; smaller picture – the wreck of *Bluebird* recovered from Coniston Water on 8th March 2001 *(Graham Beech)*

Printed by: MFP Design & Print

The Making of "The Bluebird Years"

On March 8th, 2001, more than 34 years after Donald Campbell died in his attempt to take the world water speed record past 300 mph, the wreckage of his once-beautiful *Bluebird* was brought back to the shore of Coniston Water. Witnessed by his widow, Tonia Bern-Campbell and a crowd of onlookers, the memories came flooding back. Memories for those of us who had followed Donald Campbell's exploits, and who spent their pocket money on models of his *Bluebird* car and boat – and who saw pictures of *Bluebird* streaking across Coniston Water, edging ever closer to the magic 300 mph mark. That was in the mid-1960s, the most exciting years of my life – men were orbiting the Earth – the Beatles topped the charts – and, just a few years later, Neil Armstrong walked on the Moon. Against that tapestry, I remembered watching in disbelief as *Bluebird* took to the air on her final run and cartwheeled down the lake. The powerful image of this spectacular crash has etched itself so strongly into our collective memory that young and old alike still regard Campbell as an icon.

In the middle of the year 2000, I had a call from Judith Dixon of the Bluebird Café in Coniston. For some years, she and her husband Phil had been selling a popular book by Arthur Knowles entitled 'With Campbell at Coniston' but no further copies were available. She asked if we would be interested in republishing it and this appealed to me immediately.

I was further inspired by a couple of odd coincidences. A year before Judith's call, we had published 'The Coniston Tigers' by Harry Griffin, a renowned Lakeland climber and writer – and Harry was the first newspaper reporter to break the news of Donald Campbell's fatal accident, back in 1967. Thirty-three years later, Harry's book went on to win first prize in the "Lakeland Book of The Year" competition and Border Television sent Paul Allonby to cover the event. This was a stroke of luck, as Paul had taken most of the photographs that appeared in the first edition of 'With Campbell at Coniston'. Luckily, he still had the negatives and was able to reprint the photographs for me – the new edition was starting to move along very nicely.

At first, I thought I could update the original edition simply by inserting a few extra snippets of information. This simple plan was soon scuppered, however, because of the sheer volume of information that had emerged since 1967. It was complicated still further when I learned in September 2000 of the plans to raise *Bluebird*. The new material is, therefore, presented in separate chapters, grouped into sections.

Part One is an introduction to the Campbell family and to record-breaking in general. I had the pleasure of visiting Donald Campbell's daughter, Gina, and also Ray Hewartson, Robin Brown, Geoffrey Hallawell and other members of the K7 Club (named after the registration number of *Bluebird*) who all provided me with valuable information. I made contact with Ken Norris, designer of K7, scoured the World Wide Web and soon made new friends in cyberspace, all eager to help and to put me right.

Part Two is the whole of Arthur Knowles' original 'With Campbell at Coniston', virtually unchanged, with most of the original photographs and some additional ones. Improved printing technology has enabled us to place the photographs in their optimum positions rather than bunch them in sections. A few minor textual errors have been corrected.

Part Three is a retrospective of post-1967 events. It begins with a full account of the raising of *Bluebird* by Bill Smith's team – and I was extremely fortunate to have the benefit of Bill's advice while writing this chapter. I could so easily have made so many mistakes. Next, there is a unique analysis of the crash derived from material provided by Ken Norris, followed by a history of the K7 Club based on an interview with Ray Hewartson. Then, there are details of how *Bluebird* and the Campbells have been immortalised in paintings, models, and internet web sites. Donald's single-mindedness even inspired heavy-metal band Marillion's "Out Of This World" – the lyrics being on the band's official web site, www.marillion.com. Finally, at the end of the book there is a very brief look into the future of high-speed boats.

After all the hard work in writing and revising this book, in the first few weeks of 2001, as the plans to recover *Bluebird* became public knowledge, I was privileged to correspond with Tonia, Donald's widow. Recalling the excitement and affection that they both shared, she told me how she was consoled by the fact that Donald is not forgotten and that he is still Britain's hero – and hers. We all share her sentiments and, in a small way, this book will help to preserve her husband's memory.

Acknowledgements

ARTHUR Knowles made the following acknowledgements in his original 1967 edition of *With Campbell at Coniston*: "The author is greatly indebted to Mr. Leo Villa for personal memories, technical details and confirmation of dates. The following three books were also consulted: *Into the Water Barrier* by Donald Campbell in collaboration with Alan W. Mitchell (Odhams Press, 1955); *Bluebird and the Dead Lake* by John Pearson (Collins, 1965); and *Speed on Wheels* by Sir Malcolm Campbell (Sampson Low, Marston, 1949)."

In this new edition, I am pleased to acknowledge the assistance of the following people who all helped in various ways:

David Watt – for photographs, diagrams, background material and technical advice

Ken Norris – personal reminiscences, technical data and diagrams relating to the design of *Bluebird* K7

Bill Smith – for background information on the recovery operation and for educating me on the technicalities of wreck location

Gina Campbell – hospitality, helpful information and photographs relating to the Campbell family

Paul Allonby – for researching and printing most of the photographs in this book

Ray Hewartson – historical information, a map of Coniston Water and photographs

Philip Briggs – for advice on the technicalities of speed measurement and for producing the family of speed curves in Chapter 19

Beatrice Donze of Compagnie des Montres Longines – technical information and photographs of timing equipment

The Seattle Hydroplane and Raceboat Museum – photographs and historical data

Parker Jones of Sitka, Alaska – for additional speed record data

News International – computer-enhanced photographs of *Bluebird*'s final run

Edwin Maher of the Lakeland Motor Museum – for photographs and information

I have tried to acknowledge all copyright holders. However, in a few cases it has not been possible to trace the names of photographers dating back to the 1940s and 1950s. Some of the credits refer to pictures that were re-photographed by me from their owners' collections and do not necessarily imply that the current owners are claiming copyright. All other photographs are, to the best of my knowledge, ascribed to the original photographer or the current copyright holder. If somebody's copyright has unknowingly not been acknowledged, I can only apologise – I have done my best!

Additionally, I referred to many sources of information, including the following web sites:

www.lesliefield.com
www.hydroplane.net
www.thunderboats.com

I am happy to acknowledge the background information I have been able to glean from them and I recommend them as impeccable sources of expertise and enthusiasm.

Graham Beech, Senior Partner in Sigma Press

Contents

1958: Donald Campbell with *Bluebird* and daughter Gina on the *USS United States,*
heading for record attempts on Lake Canandaigua, in New York State.

Part One

Golden Years for Record-Breakers

Graham Beech

1

Bluebirds: a family affair

HERE is a potted history of the Campbells. Much of it has been gleaned from Gina Campbell's autobiographical book *Bluebirds – the Story of the Campbell Dynasty*. Unavoidably, there is some overlap with the more extensive descriptions in Part Two, but it is hoped that by bringing together various strands, the reader will be able to learn what has driven the Campbells in their pursuit of speed.

The family traces its ancestry from the clan Campbell of Argyll. Donald's daughter, Gina, has the evidence in the shape of a broadsword that belonged to a forebear who may have fought at the Battle of Flodden Field in 1513. As an indication of her family's inclination to take charge of their own destinies, her great-great-great-grandfather left Scotland to walk the 600 miles from Tain to London. This turned out to be a wise investment of his time for, after taking part in the Battle of Waterloo, he went on to establish a successful firm of diamond merchants, and this provided a solid financial basis for future generations.

Sir Malcolm Campbell (1885-1949)

Thanks to the foresight and acumen of his ancestors, the young Malcolm Campbell, Donald's father, had all the benefits that family wealth can bring. However, he was also a successful businessman in his own right – primarily as a Lloyd's under-writer with an instinct for developing innovative insurance policies. He was able to indulge his sporting interests, and his first love was aviation. Just after Louis Blériot's cross-channel flight of 1909, he attempted to win a £1,000 prize offered to the first Englishman to fly. Unfortunately, the aircraft he built was a flop and Malcolm lost most of his money.

Undeterred, he turned to motor-racing. By 1908, he had already entered a race at the famous Brooklands circuit, near

A postcard from Daytona Beach dated 7th March 1935 showing *Bluebird* with a handwritten note recording a speed of 276.186 mph *(Gina Campbell)*

Weybridge. Success came later in the shape of a Darracq car that he found in a Kennington junk yard: a vehicle that was capable of 100 mph – a phenomenal speed in the days preceding the First World War. Just the day before a classic race at Brooklands, Malcolm went into London to see Maeterlinck's play, *The Blue Bird*, based on the story of the "blue bird of happiness" – always

YES, THINKS HE'S CAMPBELL IN HIS NEW BLUEBIRD

A picture postcard inspired by Malcolm Campbell *(photo supplied by David Watt)*

Sir Malcolm at Pendine Sands in 1927, with well-wishers *(Castrol Oil Company)*

tantalisingly close, yet forever beyond reach. He was so inspired that, overnight, the Darracq was painted blue and christened *Bluebird* – the first of all his cars and boats to bear this name.

His first attempt on the land speed record was in 1922, the year after Leo Villa joined him as his mechanic. Unofficially, Malcolm reached 135 mph at Saltburn, Yorkshire, in a 350 h.p. Sunbeam. He raised this to 146 mph in September 1924, 150.86 mph in July 1925 and then, in February 1927, to 174.88 mph – all at Pendine Sands, South Wales.

There was intense competition between Malcolm Campbell and Henry Segrave, who also raced at Brooklands. Segrave turned his attention to record-breaking and, in his 4 litre Sunbeam, raised the record at 152.33 mph in 1926. After some setbacks in Britain, Campbell decided that conditions in the United States were more conducive to record-breaking attempts. By the time he and his greatly modified *Bluebird* arrived at Daytona Beach in 1928, the record had been racked up to 203.79 mph by Segrave in a 1,000 h.p. Sunbeam. Accepting the challenge, Campbell went on to raise this to 276.88 mph at Daytona and then took *Bluebird* past the 300 mph barrier to 301.13 mph at Bonneville Salt Flats, Utah, in September 1935. By now, *Bluebird* was powered by a massive 2,500 h.p. super-charged V12 Rolls-Royce engine.

Campbell then turned his attention to water-speed records.

"August reflections" – a painting by Arthur Benjamins of Sir Malcolm Campbell's
K4 *Bluebird* boat (see page 193 for details)

His arch-rival, the newly-knighted Sir Henry , had died in 1930 when his boat hit a submerged log after setting a new water-speed record. Undeterred by this, Malcolm began his challenge to water speed records with a hydroplane called, inevitably, *Bluebird*. With this boat, designated K3, he raised the water-speed record in September 1937 to 129.5 mph on Lake Maggiore, Switzerland. A new *Bluebird* (K4) was then designed with three contact points – two at the front and one at the back – to reduce contact with the water. With this he raised the record to 141.72 mph on Coniston Water in August 1939, just before the Second World War. After the war, *Bluebird* was converted to jet propulsion, but this was unsuccessful due to problems with steering and stability. There is more to a jet hydroplane than simply swapping a propeller for a turbojet!

Donald Campbell (1921-1967)

Almost the whole of this book is about Donald Campbell and his speed record attempts, but these personal insights may be of interest. Donald followed in his father's footsteps and, to some extent, seemed always trying to live up to the image of the confident, domineering Malcolm. After a job in the City of London and then as a travelling salesman, he went into partnership with

Donald in the cockpit of the K7 *Bluebird (photo supplied by David Watt)*

the Meldrum brothers to manufacture power tools. In parallel with developing a successful business he developed a love of boats. His first craft was a simple 30-footer with a single engine, and on it he learned seamanship while reading manuals en route! He used this first boat on a sales mission to Belgium – so successfully that his next purchase, in 1949, was a much larger ex-Royal Navy torpedo recovery vessel, which he also used for overseas sales trips. All went well until it exploded in Lisbon harbour due to a fuel leak!

After the death of Sir Malcolm in 1949, Donald was attracted by the romance and excitement of high-speed boats, and the social life that went with them. Perhaps he was always trying to live up to the high profile image of his father, or to prove himself in some way. But the 1950s were also years when Britain had a much higher international standing – a time when we felt we could tackle anything and when British engineering was the envy of the world.

Donald at first decided to try his hand at powerboat racing, and only later did he turn to breaking water speed records. As is well documented in Part Two of this book, he started by buying the K4 *Bluebird* (in its jet conversion form) from his father's executors, and was probably more than a little peeved that it had not been bequeathed to him. Nevertheless, he achieved enormous success on both land and water and in 1964, perhaps at the pinnacle of his career, he raised the world land speed record to 403.1 mph in July on Lake Eyre and, in December, the world water speed record to 276.3 mph on Lake Dumbleyung – both locations being in Australia. He was the only man ever to hold both records in the same calendar year, which he achieved with just nine hours to spare.

Donald had plans for a supersonic rocket-powered *Bluebird* car, designated CN-8. He embarked on an attempt to go faster than 300 mph in his ageing but re-engined *Bluebird* K7 boat, thereby hoping to secure media interest and sponsorship to fund the CN-8 project. On January 4th 1967, he died during his return run on Coniston Water and his body was never found. A proto-type of CN-8 was built but, some time after his death, was almost certainly sold for scrap.

Donald's first marriage was to Daphne Harvey in 1945; they had one daughter, Gina, born in 1948. Daphne petitioned for divorce and was succeeded in 1952 by Dorothy McKegg, the daughter of a New Zealand dentist. Donald divorced her in 1957 and, a year later, married Tonia Bern, a Belgian-born cabaret artiste. In 1963, Tonia was quoted as saying "Before long my husband may be the fastest man on earth, or I may be a widow". Unfortunately, both of these predictions came true.

After Donald's death, Tonia returned to her cabaret career, firstly in England and then in America, where she now lives, near Los Angeles. In 1989, she married the comedy actor Bill Maynard who has lived in Yorkshire since 1997 and, sadly, suffered a stroke in 2000. On March 13th 2001, it was reported that they were reunited after Tonia came to England to see *Bluebird* being raised from Coniston Water.

Gina Campbell

Gina is of a different tempera-
ment than either her grandfather, Malcolm or her father,
Donald. Always the rebel, her
childhood could not have
been an easy one, with a
restless father obsessed with
fast boats to the exclusion of a
"normal" life – what other girl
would have to get used to a
father who kept a spare jet
engine in the garage?

Gina Campbell

Although Gina established
a strong bond with Dorothy,
Donald's second wife, her
unsettled family background
made it difficult for her to
form personal relationships.
She developed a love of animals and her first, and enduring, love
was horse riding. As a young girl, she was desperate to have her
own horse and Donald bought her one as a reward for biting her
nails less often!

Donald's record attempts took place, for the most part, while
Gina got on with her life. She recalls that, at seven years of age,
although she did not accompany her father on his 1955 trip to
Lake Mead, near Las Vegas, she has since paid a sentimental
journey to where he first thought of adding the land speed record
to his achievements. In 1958, she joined him on his next American trip on the *USS United States* for record attempts on Lake
Canandaigua, in New York State. They were there for six months
and Gina attended an American High School – a refreshingly
different experience from English boarding schools. In 1963 she
travelled to Australia, to be with Donald during his first antipo-
dean record attempts. He regularly commuted by private aircraft
between Adelaide and Lake Eyre but, on one occasion, in haste to
escape an impending storm, Gina came close to falling out of a
Piper Aztec when a door flew open at a thousand feet. She was
put off flying for years.

In addition to riding and show jumping, Gina – perhaps inevi-

Agfa Bluebird at full throttle in 1984 *(Gina Campbell)*

tably – also became interested in powerboats. This interest blossomed after she met Michael Standring – a man some years younger than her, with handsome looks, a love for life and, just as important, a liking for speed. One day, after rejecting the idea of buying another horse, Gina said to Michael "Shall we get a boat?" They bought a modest-sized ski-boat, christened it *Bluebird* (of course!) and, just like Donald, set off with an instruction manual, learning how to drive it.

This was Gina's way into the boating fraternity. In the early 1980s, she and Michael bought a 25-foot *Phantom* powerboat, with the ambition to excel at offshore racing. Finance was a major obstacle, but this was overcome when they got the backing of Agfa-Gevaert, the reprographic company. With a slight change of the boat's name to *Agfa-Bluebird* the Spithead Trophy was won by Gina in May 1984 and she went on to win the National Championship of the Royal Yachting Association in 1984 and then the European in 1985. Her next boat, *Agfa Bluebird II*, was quite different: a prop-driven catamaran designed for record-breaking attempts. With this, in 1984 Gina broke the unofficial World Ladies' water speed record at Nottingham at a measured speed of 126 mph. In her second record boat, simply

Agfa Bluebird II: Gina's record-breaking catamaran *(Gina Campbell)*

called *Bluebird*, she raised the record to 166 mph on Lake Taupo in New Zealand on 1st April 1990; by this time, the Ladies' Water Speed Record was an officially recognised category.

Gina has strong links with New Zealand – a country almost synonymous with water sports and also the home of Dorothy, Donald Campbell's second wife. Out there, in 1986, she was navigating for Glenn Urquhart when their powerboat touched the top of a wave, flipped over and then went onto its side, continuing underwater at full power. Despite – or perhaps because of this – from 1987, Gina was involved in a campaign run by the New Zealand Water Safety Council to promote public awareness of the dangers inherent in water sport and leisure.

She was again in the media spotlight when, in February 2001, plans were revealed in *The Sunday Telegraph* to raise *Bluebird* from the bottom of Coniston Water with the help of an underwater surveyor called Bill Smith who was, it was reported, an acquaintance of Gina. When the story broke, Gina was overseas and it was not possible to hear her side of the story. Further details are in chapter 18 of this book.

Don Wales

Don Wales, the nephew of Donald Campbell, is a photographer and is also involved in the quest for higher speeds – he plans to travel at more than 300 mph in a battery-powered *Bluebird* car. Don's grandfather, Sir Malcolm Campbell, set a land speed record of 174.88 mph on Pendine Sands in 1927. Over 70 years

The all-electric *Bluebird* car *(Don Wales)*

later, on 20th August 2000, Don established an official UK speed record for an electric car of 137 mph – also on Pendine Sands.

Don's electric *Bluebird* uses motors that have been turned inside out compared to a conventional design: they have magnets on the central, spinning, rotor while the coils of wire that generate the electromagnetic force, and hence the torque to turn the rotor, are on the outside. This direct-drive mechanism overcomes the approximate 5,000 revs per minute limitation of conventional electric motors which have carbon brushes pressing against the contacts of their rotors.

Motors of this type are mounted directly to each rear wheel of the electric *Bluebird* and no gearbox is required. In the future, the project team plans to attach motors also to the front wheels, thereby giving greater traction. Conventional rechargeable lead-acid accumulators are used as a 600-volt power source, but lighter batteries may give a better power-to-weight ratio. Technological advances such as these may have a spin-off for drivers of more conventional vehicles – an ecological solution to the pollution problems of the internal combustion engine.

2

Water Speed Record History

ENTIRE books have been written about water speed records, the boats that were used and the people who drove them, so this chapter is simply a brief synopsis aimed at the general reader. The tables that are included have been compiled by reference to several sources, including data published by the Speed Record Club.

Propeller-driven hydroplanes

Powerboat records can be traced from the Harmsworth Trophy races that recommenced after the First World War. The *Miss America* series were inelegant but powerful creations that raised the record to just under 100 mph, driven first by Commodore Garfield Arthur ("Gar") Wood and then by his brother, George.

A British competitor emerged in the shape of the smaller and lighter *Miss England* series, designed by Fred Cooper and sponsored by Lord Wakefield of Castrol Oil fame. In 1930, Sir Henry Segrave regained the speed record for the United Kingdom in *Miss England II*, but died later that year in a subsequent attempt to break his own record whilst travelling at an estimated 120 mph. The damaged boat was repaired and driven by Kaye Ernest Don, who broke three more records against stiff competition from the Americans. *Miss England III* (designated K1) was a further development of this series of boats, but the 120 mph barrier was ultimately broken by Gar Wood in *Miss America X*, powered by four 1,600 h.p engines.

By the beginning of the Second World War, Sir Malcolm Campbell's K3 and K4 *Bluebird* boats took the record to over 140 mph and his achievements are described elsewhere in this book.

American designers and drivers now lead the way in their

enthusiasm for propeller-driven hydroplane racing, buoyed up by successful sponsorship deals and leading-edge design and technology.

The last propeller-driven boat to hold the absolute water speed record: *Slo-mo-shun IV* on Lake Washington, 7 July 1952. *(The Seattle Times)*

One of the most successful designs was the oddly named three-pointer *Slo-mo-shun*, which was designed by Ted Jones, an employee of the Seattle-based Boeing aircraft company. This was one of the first hydroplanes to ride on a semi-submerged propeller and was hugely successful, particularly in the form of *Slo-mo-shun IV*, in which Stanley Saÿres raised the record to over 160 mph in 1950 and then to 178 mph in 1952. The next version, *Slo-mo-shun V* achieved an unenviable record of its own by turning a backward somersault at around 160 mph, landing upright and continuing without its driver, Lou Fageol, who was seriously injured.

A fondly-remembered hydroplane is *Hawaii Kai III*, built by Les Staudacher and owned by Edgar Kaiser. It inherited the engine of *Slo-mo-shun IV* after a collision which had damaged the latter's hull beyond repair. Known also as "The Pink Lady", *Hawaii Kai III* went on to raise the record to over 187 mph and, on one pass through the measured kilometre, became the first propeller-driven boat to go faster than 200 mph.

Table 1: Records for Immersed & Semi-immersed Propeller-driven craft

Speed	Driver	Craft	Date	Place
74.87 mph	Gar Wood (USA)	*Miss America*	15 September 1920	Detroit River, Michigan, USA
80.57 mph	George Wood (USA)	*Miss America II*	6 September 1921	Detroit River, Michigan, USA
92.84 mph	George Wood (USA)	*Miss America VII*	4 September 1928	Detroit River, Michigan, USA
93.12 mph	Gar Wood (USA)	*Miss America VII*	23 March 1929	Indian River, Miami, USA
98.76 mph	Sir Henry Segrave (GB)	*Miss England II*	13 June 1930	Windermere, England
102.26 mph	Gar Wood (USA)	*Miss America IX*	20 March 1931	Indian River, Florida, USA
103.49 mph	Kaye Don (GB)	*Miss England II*	2 April 1931	Parana River, Argentina
110.22 mph	Kaye Don (GB)	*Miss England II*	9 July 1931	Lake Garda, Italy
111.72 mph	Gar Wood (USA)	*Miss America IX*	5 February 1932	Indian River, Florida, USA
117.43 mph	Kaye Don (GB)	*Miss England III*	18 July 1932	Loch Lomond, Scotland
119.81 mph	Kaye Don (GB)	*Miss England III*	18 July 1932	Loch Lomond, Scotland
124.86 mph	Gar Wood (USA)	*Miss America X*	20 September 1932	St. Clair River, Algonac, USA
126.32 mph	Sir Malcolm Campbell (GB)	*Bluebird K3*	1 September 1937	Lake Maggiore, Italy
129.50 mph	Sir Malcolm Campbell (GB)	*Bluebird K3*	2 September 1937	Lake Maggiore, Italy
130.91 mph	Sir Malcolm Campbell (GB)	*Bluebird K3*	17 August 1938	Hallwiler See, Switzerland
141.74 mph	Sir Malcolm Campbell (GB)	*Bluebird K4*	19 August 1939	Coniston Water, England
160.32 mph	Stanley Sayres (USA)	*Slo-Mo-Shun IV*	26 June 1950	Lake Washington, USA
178.50 mph	Stanley Sayres (USA)	*Slo-Mo-Shun IV*	7 July 1952	Lake Washington, USA
184.49 mph	Art Astbury (CAN)	*Miss Supertest II*	1 November 1957	Lake Ontario, Canada
187.63 mph	Jack Regas (USA)	*Hawaii Kai III*	30 November 1957	Lake Washington, USA
200.42 mph	Roy Duby (USA)	*Miss U.S.1*	17 April 1962	Lake Guntersville, USA
205.49 mph	Russ Wicks (USA)	*Miss Freei.com*	15 June 2000	Lake Washington, USA

Hawaii Kai III: Jack Regas' 1957 record breaker
(Seattle Hydroplane and Raceboat Museum)

The *Miss U.S.* series had a distinctly flatter profile than most of its predecessors. The original *Miss U.S.* won the 1955 Rogers Memorial Trophy and its successor, *Miss U.S.1*, went on to break the water speed record at Guntersville, Alabama, at a whisker above 200 mph in 1962. As with *Hawaii Kai III*, the hull was built by Les Staudacher and the powerplant was a 2,200 h.p. Rolls-Royce V12 aircraft engine. Most recently, Russ Wicks in *Miss Freei.com* raised the record to over 205 mph.

The boats in Table 1 all had internal combustion (IC) piston engines except for *Miss Freei.com* which was powered by a Lycoming T-55 L-7 shaft-turbine. Boats powered by IC engines but not driving an immersed propeller are excluded – explaining the absence of *Hydrodome IV* which set a record of 70.86 mph on 9th September 1919, using an aeroplane propeller.

Jet turbine boats

The jet-powered version of Malcolm Campbell's *Bluebird* (K4) was launched in 1947 on Coniston Water; in place of its Rolls-Royce piston engine, it had a Goblin II turbojet. Speeds in excess of 200 mph were thought to be attainable – but not for K4, which repeatedly became unstable at 120 mph or so. After abandoning this version, K4 was re-converted with a Rolls-Royce type "R" piston engine.

1949: The K4 *Bluebird* at the jetty *(David Watt)*

Next in line was John Cobb's *Crusader* (K6), designed by Reid Railton. Railton's innovative design had two sponsons at the stern and a flat forward section. It was powered by a De Havilland Ghost jet engine (as used in the Comet jet airliner) with 5000 pounds thrust. Cobb was killed in a 1952 attempt on the record – he was timed at 206.89 mph on the first run but crashed on the return.

At about the same time, Frank Hanning-Lee, a naval officer and descendant of Horatio Nelson, invested £14,000 in his 1951 25-footer, *White Hawk* (K5). Much of the (largely unpaid) design work was done by Ken Norris, designer of *Bluebird*. Ken left the project before it was taken to Windermere in August 1952 for trials; initially, it was fitted with a 1943 Whittle turbojet and, later, a 6,000 h.p. Rolls-Royce Derwent. The Hanning-Lees deserved full marks for effort, but *White Hawk* was notoriously unstable and never exceeded their claimed 100 mph – and may not have gone much over 70 mph. The good news was that Frank and his glamorous wife Stella, who volunteered to drive the boat on a record attempt, survived to tell the tale – though the whereabouts of the Hanning-Lees and *White Hawk* remain a mystery.

Infinitely more successful was the K7 *Bluebird* and its records occupy much of the following table and most of the rest of this book. Donald Campbell raised his own record almost each year from 1955, encouraged by the fact that Billy Butlin, of holiday camp fame, offered an annual prize of £5,000 to anybody who broke the record. This was a good way to finance the project and may explain why the record inched up so slowly.

The current record has been held by Ken Warby since 1978. (Ken has plans to raise the record still higher – see the final chapter in this book.)

Table 2: Records for jet turbine boats

Speed	Driver	Craft	Date	Place
202.32 mph	Donald Campbell (GB)	*Bluebird* K7	23 July 1955	Ullswater, England
216.20 mph	Donald Campbell (GB)	*Bluebird* K7	16 November 1955	Lake Mead, Nevada, USA
225.63 mph	Donald Campbell (GB)	*Bluebird* K7	19 September 1956	Coniston Water, England
239.07 mph	Donald Campbell (GB)	*Bluebird* K7	7 November 1957	Coniston Water, England
248.62 mph	Donald Campbell (GB)	*Bluebird* K7	10 November 1958	Coniston Water, England
260.35 mph	Donald Campbell (GB)	*Bluebird* K7	14 May 1959	Coniston Water, England
276.33 mph	Donald Campbell (GB)	*Bluebird* K7	31 December 1964	Lake Dumbleyung, W. Australia
285.21 mph	Lee Taylor (USA)	*Hustler*	30 June 1967	Lake Guntersville, Alabama, USA
288.60 mph	Ken Warby (Aus)	*Spirit of Australia*	20 November 1977	Blowering Dam Reservoir, NSW, Australia
317.60 mph	Ken Warby (Aus)	*Spirit of Australia*	8 October 1978	Blowering Dam Reservoir, NSW, Australia

3

Timing the Records

TO qualify for a new record, the rules of the Union of International Motor Boating (UIM), now the Monaco-based Union
Internationale Motonautique, stipulate that the craft completes a
run each way through the measured mile or kilometre within
one hour and the average speed must exceed the existing record
by 0.75%. Given these stringent requirements and the high cost
of running record attempts, the accurate measurement of
elapsed time is crucial to all record-breaking attempts.

Various devices, originally based on mechanical clocks and
watches, are loosely grouped as "Chronographs" though, since
the term is derived from the Greek for "time writer", a true
chronograph should, strictly speaking, both *measure* time intervals and *record* them on a suitable medium.

The first such instrument was invented by Rieussec in 1821;
this marked time intervals by dots and dashes on a revolving
dial. Rapid developments in watchmaking ensued, resulting in
increasingly accurate hand-held stop-watches. In 1911, the
Longines company introduced the first automatic timing equipment for athletics events. This was the "string-tearing system": at
the start of a race, the athlete broke a string, causing a weight to
drop and trigger an electrical contact, thereby starting the
chronograph. At the finishing line, a second string was broken
which closed a switch and stopped the timing.

Eventually, this simple system was replaced by the use of
lightbeams and photoelectric cells which operated electrical
relays. This was more reliable than pieces of string, and the first
prototype appeared in 1945. Though successful, it was still
limited by electromechanical technology – a system that was
being outpaced by increasing competitiveness in athletics,
motor racing and, of course, speed records.

The next phase was a complete departure, with the development of the Chronocamera at the Zurich Polytechnic in the late 1940s. This contained several rotating discs, their speeds of rotation being controlled by a quartz oscillator – the natural frequency of which is a precise number of vibrations per second. Each disc was engraved with numbers, the markings on the fastest disc representing hundredths of a second. When a light beam was broken at the start or finish of an event, a flash illuminated the discs and they were instantly photographed. When commercially developed, again by Longines, this became the basis of the first chronometer to use quartz-controlled timing: something we now take for granted in almost every watch or clock.

By 1954, the Longines company – a world leader in timekeeping – had combined the Chronocamera system with a 16mm Bolex cine camera into the "Chronocinégines" instrument; this could take up to 100 photographs a second of both the discs *and* the external scene. Chronocinégines were eventually able to record time to a thousandth of a second and, in 1964, they recorded the speed of the *Bluebird II* car as it hurtled across Lake Eyre in Australia to establish a world land speed record of 403.1 mph. As can be seen in the photograph on page 29, two Chronocinégines were used at each end of the course, as is normal whenever accuracy is required, on the principle that if two complex devices show the same result, it is most unlikely that there has been any malfunction. Furthermore, by synchronising two sets of these pairs of chronometers such that they all are displaying the same absolute time, it is a simple matter to deploy one pair at the start and finish points and then to compare the time differences after the record attempt. Naturally, one inherent problem of using two separate units to measure start and finish times is that special care has to be taken as late as possible prior to use to establish that all of the units are running to the same accuracy – i.e. that they are all displaying the same time – and that they will continue to run at the same accuracy when separated from each other.

Longines chronometers were also used by the official timekeepers for Donald Campbell's water speed records. During the 1950s, mechanical chronometers were used, as seen in the photograph taken in May 1959, where conventional hand-held units are mounted in such a manner that electro-mechanically

The chronometers used to record the north-south run of *Bluebird* on 14th May 1959.
The recorded speed was 275.15 mph but the the return run reached only 245.55 mph.
The slip of paper is signed by Norman Buckley, the official timekeeper *(photo supplied by David Watt; source unknown)*

operated studs can replace the normal finger depression of the winding stem to start or stop the chronometer. Again, note the use of pairs of chronometers; the principle of their use is as for the Chronocinégines in that synchronisation of two sets of chronometers is all that is needed to determine the absolute time period from start to finish.

By their very nature, electro-mechanical devices can never be as accurate as quartz-controlled chronometers so, in November 1966, a team of official timekeepers arrived at Coniston under the supervision of Raoul Crelerot. Two Longines Chronocinégines were deployed at either end of the measured kilometre, just as they were when timing Campbell's land speed record. An auxiliary telescope was used – see photograph on page 99. This was used for two purposes. Firstly, to ensure that the line of the Chronocinégines and the fixed start or finish point had been accurately positioned and that the cameras were truly at right angles to the travelled path of the moving object. The second reason is that a high-speed ciné camera has to be brought

This dramatic 1964 picture shows two Longines technicians using the Chronocinégines to film and record Donald Campbell's *Bluebird* at over 400 mph on the dry bed of Lake Eyre in Australia *(Longines)*

up to speed gently, otherwise it will shred the film. At 100 frames per second, and with only 10 metres or so of film, this is a tricky operation; the telescope was probably aligned with a point just before the start/finish line to enable the camera to be started up, and taken up to optimum speed, just in time to photograph the start or finish event.

This film-based system has been supplanted by computer-based systems, though the principles remain much the same. For example, in 1992, Omega Electronics introduced the Scan-o-Vision system, further developed for the 1996 Atlanta Olympics as the Swatch "Hawk Eye"; this uses video cameras at the start/finish lines connected to a central PC, which can also accept other external data such as wind speed. Timing results, accurate to a thousandth of a second, can be output to a digital display and images are stored on disk for later playback.

Timing for sporting events continues to become ever more sophisticated. In motor racing, each car now has an on-board transmitter, permitting continuous measurement and display of times and speeds for both drivers and spectators.

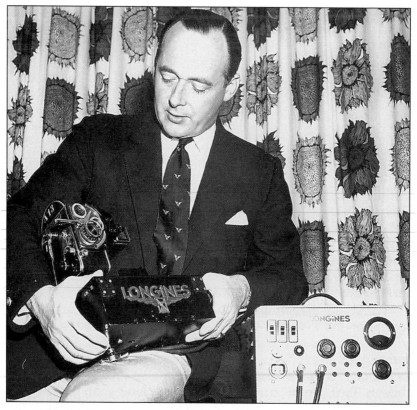

Donald Campbell at the Longines Watch Company's works in September 1966. He is pictured holding the Bolex-Paillard camera connected to the Longines Chronocinégines used to time his performances at Lake Eyre, Australia *(Longines)*

4
_____

The Building of Bluebird K7

A T high speed, a propeller-driven boat will have its bow lifted well clear of the water due to air pressure under the hull, which is being driven forwards by the propeller at the stern. All such craft are called "prop-riders". Complex design factors emerge for such boats at speeds beyond 150 mph or so. The designer tries to ensure that the propeller stays in the water, that instabilities do not set in and that the angle of the prop-riding boat does not become so great that it flips onto its back – which is exactly what happened to *Slo-mo-shun V* (see Chapter 2).

Turning a propeller in water to achieve forward motion is an inefficient process. The overall efficiency (forward kinetic energy divided by the energy output of the engine) in propeller-driven boats is typically around 25%. Believing that this could be improved upon with better aerodynamics, Donald Campbell approached Kenneth and Lewis Norris to design a streamlined but safe boat capable of a top speed of 200 mph. This was initially intended to be a two-seater prop-driven racing boat and the aim was to bring back the Harmsworth Trophy from the then American holder. For this purpose, no aerodynamic control surfaces such as tailplanes or fins are allowed.

Whilst model testing was taking place, Campbell moved the goalposts and decided to aim for a more glamorous goal: the world water speed record. Given the limitations of prop-riders and the need to achieve speeds comfortably in excess of the record of 178.5 mph held by *Slo-mo-shun IV*, jet propulsion was chosen. Two "Beryl" turbojets were provided by the Ministry of Supply, with a third lent by Cranfield College of Aeronautics.

Design considerations

A hydroplane design was selected with one rear and two forward planing surfaces. This was considered to be more stable than

BLUEBIRD K3   1937

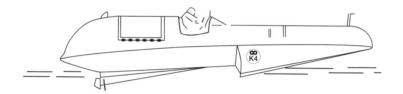

BLUEBIRD   1939 - 1950

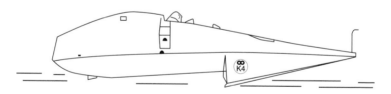

JET CONVERSION   1947

BLUEBIRD K4   1951

The K3 and K4 *Bluebird* designs *(drawings by David Watt)*

Crusader (K6) driven by John Cobb, who died when his craft became unstable and went nose-under at 200 mph. The Norris brothers also suggested the existence of a "water barrier" in which the surface of a lake may present, at high speeds, an oscillating force of the same frequency as that of the natural fore-and-aft pitching of the boat, thereby leading to a potentially catastrophic resonance. This may be similar to the resonance effect experienced by groups of people all walking in step across certain bridges. In the year 2000, London's Millennium Bridge was closed for this reason. There is, however, little evidence to support the water barrier theory and it is more a matter of designing in a resistance to the sledgehammer pounding of water on the undersurface of the hull.

In an attempt to reduce the tendency to fore-aft oscillation – and hence a possible nose-dive or back-flip – the Norris brothers carefully analysed a ciné film of *Crusader*'s last fateful run. Their conclusions were:

❏ A low centre of gravity was needed, whilst keeping the jet engine nozzle just clear of the water when static or at low speeds.

❏ The floats should have anti-dive characteristics, such that the angle of attack was steeper than usual, giving good lift at low speed and high stability in rough water.

❏ The fuel tank should be at the centre of gravity so that the trim of the craft would remain stable as fuel was consumed.

❏ A robust construction was essential to withstand possible high-frequency vibrations of the surface of the water against the hull.

The initial configuration, much the same as the final design, was based on an aerodynamic central hull with forward planing surfaces mounted on outriggers. A one-eighth scale model was constructed and this was used both in wind tunnels and in self-propelled form to assess performance and stability.

This first phase presumed that *Bluebird* was to be a competitive racing craft. With the change of policy to record-breaking, and the choice of jet power rather than prop-rider design, the Norris brothers improved the aerodynamics whilst generally reducing lift. Dynamic stability was investigated in depth using the facilities, staff and students of the aeronautics department at

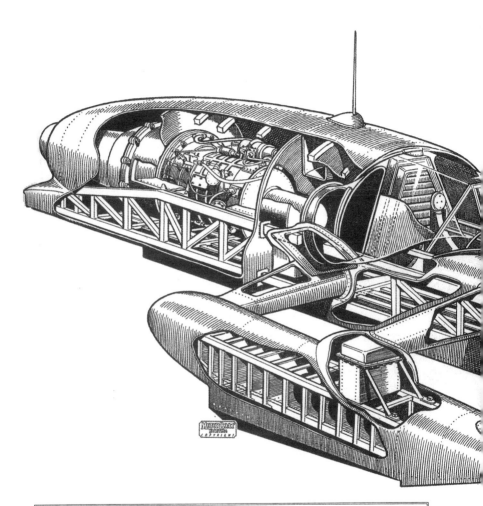

The original Bluebird
This detailed cross-section illustrates the original design of *Bluebird*,
complete with its "Beryl" jet engine, as launched on Ullswater in 1955. The
final 1965 version had a tail fin, redesigned sponsons, a smoother cockpit
canopy and an "Orpheus" engine, as illustrated elsewhere in this chapter.
*(Reproduced from the October 1955 edition of "Motor Boat and Yachting"
by kind permission of The National Magazine Company)*

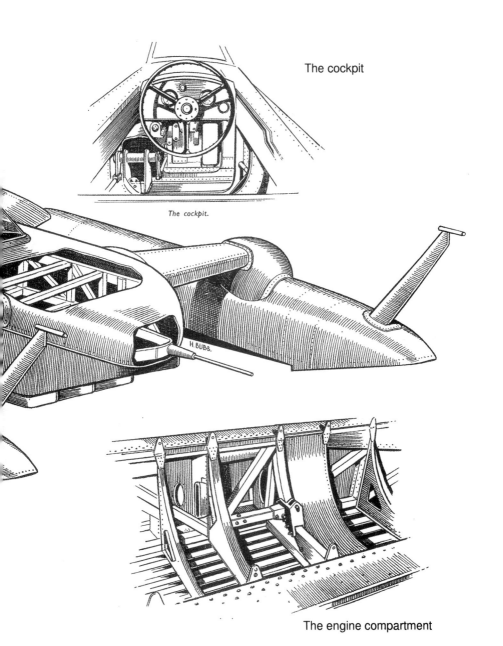

The cockpit

The cockpit.

H. BUBB.

The engine compartment

Bluebird K7
Plan area/weight 32.8lb./sq. ft.

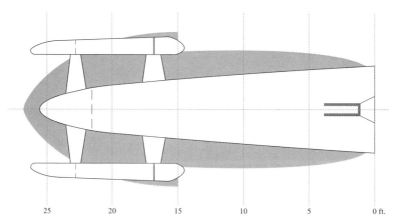

25	20	15	10	5	0 ft.

Plan views of K4 & K7, showing the "kite" airlift area of K4 (shaded) compared to K7
(based on diagrams kindly supplied by Ken Norris)

Imperial College, London, and it was found that there was ample margin of safety for estimated, scaled-up speeds up to 250 mph (see Chapter 19 for further details). Construction of a larger scale model to assess low-speed characteristics was favoured, but this was precluded by time and finance considerations.

The detailed design phase of the full-scale craft began in January 1954. It is remarkable that progress from this date was so rapid – just 18 months later, *Bluebird* K7 was hurtling down Ullswater at 202.32 mph!

From model to full-scale

After the initial design and development work, construction of *Bluebird* was handled by Samlesbury Engineering Ltd, Lancashire, a company (now part of BAE Systems plc) with experience in the construction of high-speed aircraft. Their brief was to build it to the Norris brothers design which combined enormous strength with low weight. An inner framework of chrome-molybdenum seamless square-section steel tubing was constructed by Accles and Pollock Ltd. Light-alloy sections were attached to form the contours of the hull and outer skins were riveted on to complete the construction. Some 70,000 rivets were used, in addition to lapping, welding and the use of sealants to prevent the ingress of water.

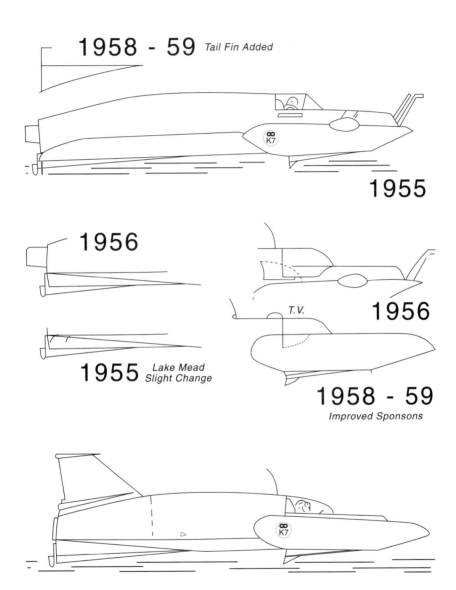

1958 - 59 *Tail Fin Added*

1955

1956

1955 *Lake Mead Slight Change*

T.V. **1956**

1958 - 59
Improved Sponsons

Changes in the design of the K7 *Bluebird* from 1955 to 1967 *(drawings by David Watt)*

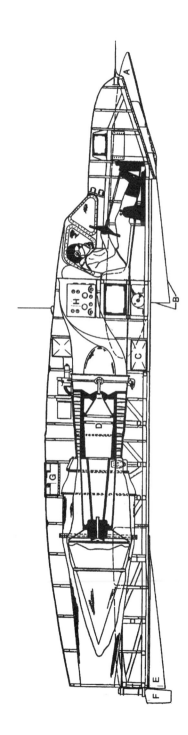

***Bluebird's* Anatomy:** A – Port float; B – Stabilizing fin; C – Segments of circular fuel tank; D – Jet engine; E – Planing shoe; F – Rudder; G – Parachute housing; H – Electronic unit automatically transmits stress factors, i.e., air speed, pitch, roll and vertical acceleration and vertical displacement of nose, to receiving unit on shore. *(Based on a diagram that appeared in 'Sports Illustrated', July 25, 1955)*

The underside consisted of a corrugated alloy surface to which two light alloy sheets were attached by 10,000 rivets to withstand buffeting from the surface of the water.

The forward floats ("sponsons") were attached to two main spars, passing at right angles through the hull. Fixed below the sponsons were the main planing shoes, machined from solid blocks of light alloy. These shoes and the rear-planing wedge on the main hull provided the three planing points for *Bluebird*, the dimensions of which were:

Overall length: 26ft 4¾in. (8.0 metres)

Overall beam: 10ft 6in. (3.2 metres)

Overall height: 4ft 8½in. (1.4 metres)

Bluebird was initially equipped with a Metropolitan-Vickers "Beryl" jet turbine with a 10-stage axial compressor; the engine itself was almost half the length of the main hull. It developed 4,000lb of thrust at 8,000 rpm and consumed 650 gallons of kerosene per hour at full power. When fully equipped, with a full load of fuel, *Bluebird* weighed about 2½ tons, over 30% of which consisted of the engine and fuel. This represented the initial design of the K7 *Bluebird*.

Test runs

Bluebird K7 arrived at Ullswater on 28th January 1955. Trials of began on Ullswater on 10th February and by 11th March speeds of up to 150 mph had been achieved. A problem was encountered at low speeds: before the craft had reached a planing condition, water spray was sucked into the engine, causing a "flame-out". This might have been avoided had larger scale models been constructed, but time and finances were at a premium. At a later stage, intake shields were added to avoid flame-out, rear buoyancy was reduced and other minor enhancements made. When testing was resumed in June 1955, higher speeds were achieved, the previous problems were overcome and on 12th July, 185 mph was reached. On the evening of Tuesday the 19th July, 1955, Donald Campbell took *Bluebird* onto what had been planned as just another test run. He slipped effortlessly past 100 mph, then accelerated spectacularly to 180 mph. He was at first euphoric, but then began to feel *Bluebird* start to slide dangerously and reported from his cockpit "I'm not enjoying this," followed by "I'm getting one hell of a ride!" However, at this stage, he had unofficially broken the existing world record without trying too hard, and the Beryl engine was not yet operating at full power. The timekeepers were called in and, on 23rd July on Ullswater, two runs of 189.57 mph and 215.08 mph gave a world record speed of 202.32 mph.

Later that year, *Bluebird* was taken to Lake Mead, Nevada, where it sunk while on test. It was recovered, repaired, and went on to a record-breaking 216.20 mph on 16th November.

In September 1956, the *Bluebird* team returned to England, this time to Coniston Water, which provided a longer straight stretch of 4½ miles on its total length of 5¼ miles. This was deemed necessary as *Bluebird* may have needed a two-mile acceleration run, and perhaps a mile to slow down safely.

Over the next four years, with the record being raised still higher, modifications were made to K7 to improve both speed and stability. By 1956 a shaped canopy replaced the original sharp-edged one and the sponsons had been altered several times. On 19th September 1956, two runs of 286.78 mph and 164.48 mph gave an average of 225.63 mph and the record had been broken again. The 286.78 mph figure remained the fastest single run for *Bluebird* until 4th January 1967.

In 1958 and 1959 the sponsons were deepened, a small tail fin was added, the air-speed indicators on the floats were removed and a single indicator placed on the rear fin. Finally, in 1965, the engine was replaced with a Bristol-Siddeley Orpheus from a Gnat jet fighter plane with 5,000lb thrust – some 25% more than the Beryl. It was in this form that *Bluebird* finally made its ultimately tragic attempt to break through the 300 mph barrier.

As a footnote: in March 2001 a copy of a book by Donald Campbell and Ken Norris was in the news. Written in 1954, it includes drawings of the various prototypes that led to the design of *Bluebird* . The copy was discovered by Eddie Yates, a Royal Navy chief petty officer.

Bluebird on Coniston Water, with snow-covered mountains as the backdrop
(Paul Allonby)

Part Two

With Campbell at Coniston

Arthur Knowles

Arthur Knowles (1915-1989)

This section of 'The Bluebird Years' is the entire text of 'With Campbell at Coniston' – including the Foreword by Leo Villa, Donald Campbell's Chief Engineer. The text is unedited apart from the correction of a few minor typographical errors. Written by Arthur Knowles and published by William Kimber in 1967, it has remained the classic contemporary account, documenting Donald Campbell's attempt to break his own water speed record and to raise it to 300 mph during the winter of 1966/7.

The author was a Lake District man whose association with the Campbells began when his father came to know Sir Malcolm Campbell during his motor racing days at Southport. For the entire nine weeks leading up to the final tragedy of 4th January 1967, Arthur Knowles was at Coniston with the Bluebird team and the press. He worked closely with Donald Campbell in preparing to write what they both hoped would be the story of Campbell's greatest triumph. As the days passed, he got to know this very private and complex man better than almost anybody else.

Knowles also understood the powerful bonds which existed between the Campbell family, water speed records, and the people of Coniston. Even those with little interest in the technology of high speed machines will be fascinated by this gripping account of the nuts and bolts of mounting a record attempt in the late 1960s. The author evokes the freezing winter mornings, the humour, the setbacks and the sheer tedium which sometimes almost overwhelmed them, as well as recalling the involvement of the whole nation in the events on the lake. Arthur Knowles wrote a book that has become a permanent memorial to the technical achievements of Bluebird's designers and engineers. More than this, the book provided a simple, unadorned record of the extraordinary courage of her driver, Donald Campbell.

Foreword to the First Edition

by Leo Villa

Formerly Chief Engineer to Sir Malcolm Campbell and Donald Campbell

I have been privileged to write a foreword to "With Campbell at Coniston" written by Mr Arthur Knowles. Donald Campbell entered my life in 1922 when he was 4½ months old. Through the passing years Donald portrayed the image of his father, inheriting the determination, courage and spirit of adventure that proclaims them outstanding and an inspiration to the younger generation of the world. Fearing for Donald's safety, his father made every effort to dissuade him from becoming interested or involved in anything to do with racing or speed attempts of any nature.

Sir Malcolm passed away through illness at the close of the year 1948 and it was at this period that Donald approached me and asked if I would join him so that he could carry on where his father had terminated, in an endeavour to keep the flag flying and retain the water speed record for England. He told me that Henry Kaiser, the American ship builder, was constructing a craft in which he hoped to recover the water speed record for the USA. At the time I warned Donald of the hazardous task he had undertaken, but stated that I would be with him through thick and thin.

Thinking back over the past years, I recall that Donald's earlier trial runs with Sir Malcolm's old *Bluebird* hydroplane caused me a great deal of anxiety, as this craft was powered by a Rolls-Royce aero engine developing approximately 2500 horsepower and was propeller driven. *Bluebird* was quite a handful.

I was soon to learn that my fears were unfounded. Donald mastered the technique after very few trial runs, and drove *Bluebird* superbly on the many more serious runs that were to follow. His father would indeed have been proud of him.

The tenacity Donald showed during his early record bids amazed me and still does, throughout a series of heartbreaking setbacks, due to experimental and mechanical failures, restricted financial resources and long delays waiting for that ever elusive safe water condition. It was after many modifications had been carried out in order to raise the record to 150 mph plus, that Stanley Sayres of America had beaten Sir Malcolm's old record of 141 mph and raised it to 176 mph in 1950. This unforeseen event had placed the record beyond any maximum the old *Bluebird* could achieve and all our spirits at that time were at a very low ebb indeed. Donald, undaunted, decided to convert *Bluebird* from a 'three pointer hydroplane' to a 'prop rider', this being the term used for the new configuration that Stanley Sayres had employed.

On completion of these modifications, the *Bluebird* was taken to Lake Garda to compete in the Oltranza Cup and at the same time regain the water speed record for Britain. Donald won that race by a substantial margin but instability at speeds over 150 mph prevented us from regaining the record on that occasion.

In 1951 *Bluebird* was taken back to Coniston for further modification and a further onslaught to regain that record. The modifications to *Bluebird* had also included a second cockpit for a riding mechanic, and my confidence in Donald's ability prompted me to ride with him on all these later trials. One morning during October 1951 I was with Donald on *Bluebird* doing a speed in excess of 170 mph when we had the misfortune to strike a submerged railway sleeper. The impact caused *Bluebird* to gyrate, slide and bounce all over the place, but I shall never forget the cool and calm way Donald mastered that frightening situation. His chief worry was for my safety.

Over the ensuing years we enjoyed many successes together and his charming personality and many great achievements brought him worldwide fame, but he always remained the modest boy we had grown to like so many years ago. He was at his best in the face of adversity and all of us who had the privilege of working with him felt we could never do enough for the 'Skipper' who gave of his best on every occasion.

Mr Knowles spent the major part of his time with us during the nine weeks of our last endeavour at Coniston and reading his tribute to Donald has given me much pleasure. I trust his book will be widely read and feel sure it will imprint a permanent memory of a very determined and courageous Englishman.

Leo Villa, 1967

5

Over a Beer in the Tavern

I had just been accused of fusing all the lights in Earls Court.
Not in so many words, but judging by the hard, long looks I was
receiving it was quite obvious what they were thinking.

It was the day before the opening of the 1950 British Indus-
tries Fair, and I had just wired up a plug to a small lamp for use in
the office behind my company's stand. As I pushed the plug
home into its socket – in that split second – all the lights went
out. I left them to their uncharitable thoughts and went to seek
some beer. After all, I had wired up hundreds of plugs in my
time ... As I walked down the main hall the lights came on again
and an apology was broadcast over the P.A. I almost turned to go
back, but my old friend John Shorrock, sales manager on a
competitor's stand, caught up with me:

"Come on – I'm going for one."

As we entered the Tavern, a voice called:

"John old sport, how are you?"

John turned in the direction of the voice and grinned.

"Donald – well, well. How nice to see you." And to me, "Come
and meet one of nature's gentlemen."

It was Donald Campbell. We joined him at his table, and
stayed with him for perhaps an hour, He was at Earls Court that
day in connection with some engineering concern; he was flying
off somewhere the following day, and felt like 'putting up his feet
for a while'. He had my complete sympathy, for the concrete
floors of the exhibition hall had played havoc with my own feet.

We discussed the various products of our respective companies, and during the conversation he turned to me and said:

"You're north country, aren't you, old boy?"

When I told him that I hailed from Southport, he said he knew
the town; his father used to drive his cars there during the days of
the sand-race meetings. And I was able to tell him that my father

had known the then Captain Campbell very well indeed. As a manager at the factory which produced Vulcan vehicles and Lea-Francis cars, he had shown the racing driver around the works one day, and I told Donald of his father's amusement when, having examined a new type of double-decker bus, he was told that it could not be driven out of the factory until a wall had been removed and a new exit made.

At the mention of Lea-Francis, Donald spoke of Kaye Don; I told him that Don's famous 'Hyper-Leaf' car, with which he won the Ulster Trophy, had been made in Southport and that as a boy I had been its first passenger on a trial run around the Marine Drive.

We spoke of men like Kaye Don, Earl Howe, 'Tim' Birkin – and Sir Henry Segrave, against whom Donald's father had battled, and I told him I had been present when Segrave had been killed on Windermere. I remember that his very pale blue eyes looked pensive for a moment – and then, with a quick change of mood; he asked:

"Did you collect any ping-pong balls, old boy?"

He meant the hundreds of these balls with which the buoyancy bags, built into Segrave's hydroplane *Miss England,* were filled. When the boat crashed the balls floated to the surface and were collected as souvenirs by the onlookers. Many can still be seen in homes to this day.

Saying goodbye to him in the main hall, we watched the slim, immaculately dressed man walk briskly away, and John murmured.

"He'll kill himself, too, one day."

When I next saw Donald Campbell he was surrounded by relatives and friends. It was in February 1955, and the scene was Ullswater. I was enjoying a climbing-cum-business holiday in Langdale and, learning that Donald was at Glenridding, I drove over the Kirkstone Pass from Ambleside, arriving just in time to see a bottle of champagne cracked against the hull of a very odd looking craft. It was the *Bluebird* which was to play such a major part in the writing of the Donald Campbell saga, and she had just been christened.

Although I saw him take her out for the first time, I did not see her at speed. It was my last day in the Lakes, and I had to leave for home. I followed their progress with considerable interest however, during the years which intervened until I saw and spoke to him again.

* * * *

What sort of man was this Donald Campbell? Why, when he could have spent a comfortable existence as 'something in the city' did he opt for a life of speed, a life in which disaster must always be imminent? Why had he foresworn the bowler hat and the pinstripe trousers for the crash-helmet and the racing overalls?

Perhaps it was inevitable, for he was of course the son of Sir Malcolm, the man in whose shadow he was to walk all his life. Not all sons follow in their fathers' footsteps, but then how many sons have fathers who are world record-breakers *and* national heroes? And the young Donald worshipped his father and was intensely proud of him.

Sir Malcolm, acknowledged master of all record-breakers, achieved nine land speed records and held the water speed record three times. When, on Daytona Beach in 1931, he captured the world land speed record for his country, he received a knighthood. For he was a typical product of his time, and at that time public interest in such achievements was tremendous. It was an age which treated its heroes handsomely and gave them due recognition. His success came when the world cried out for heroes. He fought his battles against the other giants of the day; they duelled, using cars and boats as their weapons.

In 1935 at Salt Lake in America, young Donald saw his father become the first man to travel at 300 mph. In his book *Into the Water Barrier* he described the new car which was taken to Salt Lake as one of the most beautiful machines ever built.

Perhaps the first tentative thought that he might, one day, wear the mantle of his famous father, came to the boy's mind that day as he watched him gain the world record at a speed of 301 mph. Certainly he had evidence of the dangers of such a life; on one run at 304 mph *Bluebird* burst a tyre, and his father was very close to death. Perhaps a decision was made there, as Donald stood, shielding his eyes from the glare of the sun's reflection on the salt. And perhaps his fate was decided there.

Having realised his ambition of driving *Bluebird* at 300 mph, Sir Malcolm began to turn his thoughts and his attention to speedboats. No stranger to water as a medium of travel, he owned yachts, loved to sail and taught his son to love it too. Now he looked at the possibility of regaining the water speed record held by America. It had been gained by Gar Wood at a speed of 124.80 mph.

So the first *Bluebird* boat (K3) came to be created. She was designed by T.S. Cooper and built by Saunders-Roe. Constructed of wood, she was built on the single step hydroplane principle. The same engine which had powered the car at Salt Lake was installed in her, and she was driven by a single propeller. *Bluebird* was launched and given her first trials on Loch Lomond.

On Lake Maggiore in Italy in August 1937, Sir Malcolm, with his new boat, beat Gar Wood's record by just five miles per hour. Dissatisfied with this he took *Bluebird* to Hallwiler See on the German frontier, but only succeeded in adding one mile an hour to the record. During his journey home he was already deep in the discussion of plans for the building of yet another new boat.

True to the Campbell drive and urge, these plans went ahead and a new *Bluebird* (K4) was designed by Reid Railton and built this time by Vospers. She was again powered by the same engine. When the time came for her launching Sir Malcolm decided that Donald should christen her.

In August 1939 at Coniston, the boy, having first carefully rehearsed the christening ceremony, stood near the gleaming *Bluebird* and, with his father at his side and a huge crowd gathered around, he declared:

"I name this boat *Bluebird*. May God bless her, her pilot and all who work with her."

On the Saturday of that same week, Sir Malcolm piloted his new craft along the surface of Coniston Water at a speed of 141.74 mph, and set up a new world record. This was the year which saw the outbreak of war, and all Sir Malcolm's plans for future record attempts then had to be shelved.

Early in 1940 Donald applied for pilot training in the RAF and, during his 'medical', he lied when asked by the doctor:

"Have you ever had rheumatic fever?"

"No," said Donald as firmly as he could. But it was of no avail. The chairman of the Flying Medical Board sent for him and told him that the board knew of his having contracted rheumatic fever as a boy; they were sorry, he said, but they could not allow him to fly. Donald had contracted the fever in 1937 during his days at Uppingham School and for four months had spent life in a wheelchair.

He was very distressed at the decision of the RAF to reject him, since nothing else in the services appealed to him. He chose engineering and worked in this field throughout the war, serving also as a special constable.

Soon after the end of the war, Sir Malcolm began to convert *Bluebird* into a jet powered boat. The Americans, he felt, would soon be thinking in terms of record-breaking again, and he wished to be ahead of them. However, his eyes began to cause him trouble and much of his old fire and enthusiasm left him. He continued with the conversion of the boat and this was duly completed. But when water trials were held she proved to be 'a brute of a thing and thoroughly unstable.'

There were to be no more records for Sir Malcolm Campbell. At three minutes to midnight on December 31st 1948, he died. He was laid to rest at Chislehurst and at his memorial service in St. Margaret's, Westminster, every pew was filled.

He died a wealthy man, wealth accrued not only from his record-breaking, but from his own business acumen and ability.

* * * *

Donald did not inherit the two *Bluebirds;* the car and the boat. He had to purchase them at values placed on them by the auctioneers of his father's property. It would seem, however, that he did inherit Leo Villa.

Leo, who joined Captain Campbell – as he then was – as chief mechanic in 1921, also became young Donald's guardian angel throughout the years of his childhood. Whenever the boy walked in fear of his father's wrath because of some misdemeanour, he shielded the boy from a quick tanning. He had been a page boy in a London restaurant, but he hated the job. His ambition was to be a mechanic, to work with tools and machinery. When he started to throw such things as peach melbas and inkwells at the chief chef and head porter, his father took the hint and took the boy away, telling him to go and be a mechanic.

Jules Foresti, the Italian racing driver took Leo on as his assistant. These were the days when Foresti and Captain Campbell were competing regularly at Brooklands, and Campbell bought two of the Italian's cars. When Leo brought them over from Paris and delivered them, the two men took a liking to each other; Leo joined the Campbell 'stable'. He became absolutely indispensable, and was regarded as one of the family. When Sir Malcolm died, he stayed on with Donald as engineer, friend and mentor.

Not very long after the death of his father, Donald was sitting in the study of the family home talking to 'Goldie' Gardner, the racing motorist. Gardner told him, casually, that Henry Kaiser, builder of the wartime Liberty boats, had built an Allison-engined speedboat called *Aluminium First*, with which he planned to wrest the world water speed record from Britain. He described the boat to Donald, and said:

"Guy Lombardo will be driving it, Don – and he's after the old man's record."

After Gardner had left, Donald sat brooding over his father's past achievements; the more he thought about them and considered the possibility of the Americans beating his water speed record, the angrier he became. "To hell with Kaiser," he thought. "The old man's work isn't going to be wasted."

He left the house to find Leo, who was working in the garage. He told him the news about Kaiser, and said:

"I'll give Kaiser a run for his money – I'll have a crack at it myself."

Leo eyed the excited Donald quizzically.

"It's no easy job, Don. Er – do you think . . . ?"

The two men stared at each other, then burst out laughing. The decision was reached. Donald would take over where his father had left off.

So the mantle of the great Sir Malcolm, that day in 1949, fell fairly and squarely on the shoulders of his son, and Leo Villa once more took up his position, firmly at the side of a Campbell.

*   *   *   *

Sir Malcolm had started his career as a record-breaker with years of experience behind him. Racing cars had been his dominating interest, and he had graduated from such tracks as Brooklands and Pendine Sands to the vast salt flats at Salt Lake.

Donald, however, could call on no such experience. He had been a mere witness of his father's exploits and had driven nothing faster than the family car. He made a remarkable decision that day.

6
_____

"It's a Piece of Cake"

BLUEBIRD, the second boat to bear the name, was sent down to Vospers in Portsmouth. She had been built there in 1938 as a screw-propelled boat and Donald, knowing that she had not taken at all kindly to jet propulsion, decided that she should be reconverted to her original design.

"We'll use one of the old man's Rolls engines, Leo," he said. "Probably the R37 which powered the car at Salt Lake."

The high cost of staging record bids was brought home very forcibly to Donald when the search for the old engines began. He found that his father had sold them in 1947, together with his first boat, to a dealer. He had received about £150 for the lot. Donald started negotiations with the dealer which went on for three weeks. In the end, in order to obtain the engines, gear box and drive shafting, he had to buy the old hull complete. He also had to part with the *Bluebird* car, for the dealer insisted on having it as part of a hard bargain. It was a very unhappy decision for young Donald to have to make.

However, in spite of difficulties, snags and delays, *Bluebird*, painted in gleaming sapphire, was transported to Coniston, and housed on the lakeside under tarpaulins. Donald and his team installed themselves at the Black Bull, and renewed acquaintanceship with Mrs Connie Robinson, who ran the hotel with her husband, and whom Donald had known in his father's day.

The year was 1949, and the Lake District was enjoying a wonderful summer: blue skies and hot sunshine. However, just as Donald, after a week of hard work, prepared to give *Bluebird* her first run, the weather broke. The wind rose, the rain poured down in torrents and the surface of Coniston Water was whipped to white horses.

At last, two weeks later, the wind abated, the rain stopped, and August 10th dawned still, clear and calm. *Bluebird*, with the 'new boy' in the cockpit, was towed out into the lake. After months of planning and frustration, Donald was ready to go.

Leo peered quizzically at him from the towing launch before casting off the lines.

"Good luck, Don," he said. "Take it easy."

Donald grinned, touched the throttle, and *Bluebird* was away.

He returned to the hotel that night, thrilled with his first experience.

"It's a piece of cake, Leo," he said. "What the hell were we worried about?"

The following day, a day of clear skies and a calm lake, Donald decided to 'have a go'. In spite of Leo's protestations, he was determined to give *Bluebird* her head – and he had his first taste of the dangers of this game he had chosen to play.

On his first run down the lake, *Bluebird's* port plane dipped suddenly, she swerved and slewed round to starboard. Donald had the horrible feeling that the whole lot was going over. He sweated and felt very frightened. Then as he struggled with her to regain control, he spotted a water-logged tree branch – perhaps a hundred yards away. He wrenched at the wheel, *Bluebird* snaked and skated, and the log passed – safely – a few feet away. Donald felt he had had quite enough for one day and he motored *Bluebird* very sedately back to the slipway. He climbed out of the cockpit and stared at Leo, who was giving him an 'old fashioned' look.

"Leo," he said, "this job's bloody dangerous."

He was back in the cockpit the following day, and *Bluebird* behaved herself He took her up to 145 mph, faster than his father's record, and his confidence was restored. Returning to the slipway he decided to send for the timekeepers and observers, and to go for the record without further delay.

On Wednesday, August 23rd, he believed he had got the record. After two hectic runs, during which he had narrowly missed colliding with a press launch, he returned to the slipway to be greeted with the news that he had beaten his father's record. So confident were the timekeepers that the news was broadcast by the BBC at 8 am.

However, it was not to be. The timekeepers later discovered an error, and Donald's aggregate speed was found to be some two miles per hour under the record. He and the team were bitterly disappointed; the decision was made to take *Bluebird* back home, to overhaul her and to return the following year.

They were all pleased to learn, on returning home, that Henry Kaiser's boat had been found to have a top speed of only 128 mph. If they had not succeeded in improving on Sir Malcolm's record, then neither had the Americans.

In June 1950, *Bluebird* and the team were back in Coniston; they were greeted with the news that an American, Stanley Sayres, had broken the water speed record at 160.23 mph. They were despondent, for they knew from tests that at 160 mph *Bluebird* would probably roll on her back.

Nevertheless, they persisted with trials. They constructed a second cockpit to the right of Donald's, so that Leo could travel with him to study the boat's performance, and they also installed a new propeller and drive-shaft. Full of confidence as a result of these trials, they sent for the timekeepers, determined to go for Sayer's record.

But it was not to be. *Bluebird's* engine gave trouble, her planing position left much to be desired and, after months in Coniston, the team returned home in November.

During the early months of 1951, *Bluebird* had her propeller system redesigned, her engine moved some six feet forward, and new cowlings were made to conform to the new engine position. Two new cockpits were installed, for the value of maintaining the boat as a two-seater was agreed. In May *Bluebird*, Donald and the team were at Lake Garda in Italy to compete for the Oltranza Cup – a memorial trophy to the late Sir Henry Segrave.

The race for the cup was between Donald, with *Bluebird*, and Norman Buckley, of the Windermere Motor Boat Racing Club, in his hydroplane *Miss Windermere*. After a false start, and a hair-raising four laps, Donald won the cup.

In September, after much modification to *Bluebird*, Donald took her back to Coniston with the firm intention of making another attempt on the world record. He was elated when, on one of her runs, her airspeed indicator needle swung up to 170 mph. He felt sure the record could now be regained.

But yet again, fate decreed otherwise. During a very fast run, *Bluebird* shuddered, skidded and slowly drifted to a standstill. Water poured into the engine housing; the boat sank deeper and deeper into the water, until she was submerged. That was the end of *Bluebird*. She was recovered from the lake, was examined and found to be beyond repair. They broke her up there on the lake shore.

In 1952, Stanley Sayres improved his own world record and achieved a speed of 178.497 mph. Two months later, on Loch Ness, in an attempt to recover the record for Britain, John Cobb was killed in his jet-powered boat *Crusader*.

In spite of his distress, Donald felt spurred on to continue the fight and turned his own thoughts to the idea of jet propulsion. And it was at this time that he first met, and became increasingly more closely associated with, the Norris brothers, Lewis and Kenneth. These men, brilliant engineers, designed the new jet-powered *Bluebird*; when Saunders-Roe advised Donald that they were no longer interested, and that they disagreed with his choice of jet engine, the Norris brothers became responsible for the actual building of the boat, the third boat to bear the name *Bluebird*.

She was finally launched at Ullswater in February 1955 and I was happy to be there to see the christening.

The new boat was powered by a Beryl jet engine, the unit used to power the Saunders-Roe flying boats and Donald was to find that very different techniques were needed to handle her. However, he still had not managed to capture a world record and he was a very determined young man. He accepted the problems presented by the new boat. Accepted them and solved them.

In July 1955, Donald Campbell piloted *Bluebird* along the surface of Ullswater at a speed of 202.32 mph, and became the fastest man in the world on water. All the frustrations and the heartbreak were forgotten. The breakthrough had been achieved – but this was only the beginning. In November of that same year, he took *Bluebird* to America, to Lake Mead, and he pushed his speed up to 216.02 mph. He beat the Americans on their own ground.

In the next eight years he gained five more water speed records. On Coniston Water in 1956 his speed was 225.63 mph; in 1957, 239.07 mph; in 1958, 248.62 mph; and in 1959, 260.33 mph, all on Coniston. *Bluebird*, during the four years it took to achieve this speed, was modified considerably. The height of her spars was increased, the design of her sponsons altered, and a new cockpit canopy was designed and fitted.

In Australia, on Lake Dumbleyung, in 1964, he persuaded *Bluebird* to travel at a speed of 276.33 mph. And this year proved

Donald Campbell at Glenridding pier just before the 1955 record bid, discussing the construction of a slipway for *Bluebird* with, right, Sir Wavell Wakefield, founder of Castrol Oils and owner of Ullswater Steamers, and Mr Tom Craig, a local joiner *(Alec Fraser)*

to be a memorable one, for he became the fastest man in the world, both on water and on land.

His dream of achieving the 'double' came to him at Lake Mead, in 1955, and in that year he commenced plans to build a record-breaking car. She was to be revolutionary, powered by an aircraft gas-turbine engine, and building this car became an obsession with him. He sank all his own money into it and persuaded some sixty British firms to make contributions towards its cost. When her building was finally completed, she was seen to be the most sophisticated car in the world, a mobile laboratory, and she cost about £35,000.

In 1960 Donald took the car to Utah, in America, in a glare of publicity. This was the car to end all cars and the record was a foregone conclusion: so thought Donald, his backers and the press. But, travelling at a speed of 360 mph, it crashed dramatically and Donald was badly knocked about. Amongst other injuries he suffered a skull fracture and contusion of the brain.

Lying in his hospital bed, he held a press conference and

September 1956: *Bluebird* arriving at Coniston. Note the "flying horse" logo denoting the Mobil Oil Company as a sponsor at this stage *(David Watt)*

September 1956: *Bluebird* on Coniston Water, Leo Villa in the cockpit *(David Watt)*

Bluebird on Ullswater: the setting for his July 1955 record run of 202.32 mph
(Alec Fraser)

announced that he was quite prepared to have another go at the record. So yet another *Bluebird* car was created. Sir Alfred Owen, the industrialist, was so impressed with the Campbell courage, that he built the new car for him. It followed the same basic design as the original, but with the addition of a large tail-fin like that of an aircraft.

Still suffering from the effects of his crash injuries, Donald took the new car to Australia in 1963. It was a disastrous year for him. Everything went wrong. He was accused by Sir Alfred of mismanaging the project. Donald sued and Sir Alfred withdrew. He was hammered by the Australian press. He was bedevilled by appalling weather. And Stirling Moss said at a press conference that, in his opinion, Campbell was not up to driving the car. The attempt was called off in May.

In 1964, when Donald planned a return to Australia, his backers withdrew. British industry seemed to have lost confidence in him. Nevertheless, Donald went back to the dried-up salt bed of Lake Eyre, almost entirely at his own expense; and again he ran into trouble.

Donald returned to base after a run at about 320 mph complaining of a high-frequency vibration in the car. Andrew Mustard, who was there as reserve driver for the car, was sceptical.

"I believe Campbell is scared, and when a man's as scared as he is the slightest trouble gets magnified out of all proportion."

This meant another bad press for Donald; although he treated Mustard with disdain and went on to take the record at a speed of 403 mph, much of the mud stuck; the criticisms seemed to be remembered more than the achievements.

Perhaps Donald's greatest year was 1955, after his water speed record of 216 mph. He received a wonderful press, was decorated by the Queen and was presented with a golden urn by the Las Vegas Chamber of Commerce, recording his 'courage and scientific achievement'. He was lionised everywhere he went and the Campbell star was very much in the ascendant.

Perhaps he should never have built his cars. Perhaps it was all a great mistake. He never liked them; he distrusted them and never felt 'part of the machine' as he did in the *Bluebird* boat. Certainly it was the cars which contributed to his fall in popularity and caused his star to wane. In spite of all this, however,

October 1956: a high-speed run on Coniston Water *(David Watt)*

1959: by now a small tail fin had been added to *Bluebird* and the sponsons were deeper.
Note the bulge above the cockpit, to accommodate a TV camera *(David Watt)*

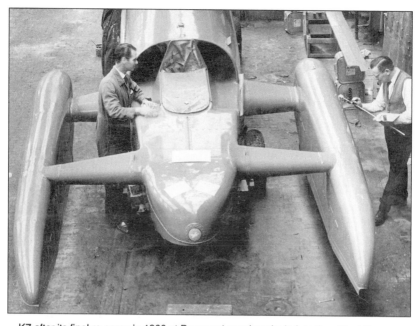

K7 after its final re-spray in 1966 at Bourners' coachworks in Lancing, West Sussex. Ray Trigwell (right) was the Master Signwriter who painted the Union Jacks and logos on K7. Note the blank white areas on the front of the boat ready to receive the red and blue crosses. *(Sussex Photo Agency)*

something in his make-up drove him on, for in 1966 plans were on the drawing board for a car of very advanced design, to be capable of supersonic speeds.

On Sunday, October 30th, 1966, Donald Campbell announced that he was returning to Coniston Water with his jet boat *Bluebird*. "I hope," he said, "to push the present speed of 276.33 mph to something nearer 300 mph."

There was no great splash of headlines. Apart from a few throw-away paragraphs in one or two papers, no one seemed to give a damn. Why then was he doing it? Why, in these days when astronauts were reaching for the stars, when submariners were searching the depths, and when the crashing of sound-barriers was a daily occurrence, was Donald Campbell returning to Coniston with a twelve-year-old boat, hoping to push it along the surface at 300 mph?

"Because," he said, "the Americans are spending millions of dollars trying to get this record from Britain. The way to beat them is to bump it out of their reach before they even get started."

7

Arrival at Coniston

THE residents of the English Lake District know all about water speed record-breakers. The craftsmen working in the boat-yards at Bowness-on-Windermere are skilled in the arts of building fast hydroplane boats, for they have built them, and improved on them, over a period of many years. The Windermere Motor Boat Racing Club holds regular race meetings on the lake during the summer months. The most famous of these boats, *Miss Windermere V*, and her predecessors are berthed only five minutes from my home at Windermere. They belong to Mr Norman Buckley, solicitor and hotelier, a great personal friend of Donald Campbell, against whom he raced in 1951 in an earlier *Miss Windermere*, for the Oltranza Cup. Norman is himself a record holder; he has captured the one-hour records on many occasions and in the spring of 1966 he won the three-hour record.

Almost opposite *Miss Windermere's* boathouse and within sight of my own window, Sir Henry Segrave made his own attempt on an early water speed record in his hydroplane *Miss England*. The boat struck a floating log and crashed; the mechanic was killed outright and Sir Henry died soon afterwards in a house on the Lancashire banks of the lake.

Donald's father, Sir Malcolm, was a regular visitor to Coniston Water on his record attempts and Donald himself kept up the tradition. After his record on Ullswater in 1965, he too came to Coniston to capture four more records.

So it was not as a stranger that he came again, in November 1966, to the scene of his past triumphs and he was made welcome. The people of Coniston loved the Campbells, and Donald in particular.

The village, in the Lake District National Park, lies a short distance from Coniston Water, at its northerly end and on the western shore. A pleasant place, nestling at the feet of the Old Man, Dow Crags and Yewdale, fells much loved by the climbers and walkers who visit them each year. The summits, the old disused copper mines, and the hobby of searching for the local semi-precious stone, the garnet, have a fascination all their own.

The villagers cater for these visitors in the summer months and provide them with three hotels, a number of guest houses, a few shops and boating facilities. When the dead leaves of autumn have fallen and the bracken turned russet, when the boots, the anoraks and the cars have left, then Coniston in winter prepares to snooze.

Not in the winter of 1966/67, however. Coniston extended her season; the hotels had an unexpected boost; the snack bars were kept busy; and the car parks were full.

After the ancient Britons had ceased to sail their coracles on the waters of the lake, came the Romans, the Norsemen, the Saxons and the Normans, and all left their mark on the place. Later still came Ruskin to live at Brantwood on the eastern shores of the lake. And in more modern times came Arthur Ransome, whose relatives still live in the area, to write his *Swallows and Amazons.* They too left their mark. And the Campbells came, to leave theirs.

The little snack bar on the beach where the boats are hired out is called 'The Bluebird Café'. The hotel and café walls in the village bear photographs of the various *Bluebirds* at speed, many of them signed by Donald. Local bank balances too, must have felt the mark of the Campbells, for the followers and chroniclers of record attempts came to Coniston and spent their money.

Coniston Water is a beautiful lake, bounded on its eastern shore by the slopes of Grisedale Forest – scene of the film *The One Who Got Away* – and, to the west, by the Lancashire Fells, with the Old Man dominating them all. I have seen it in all its many moods; sometimes it can look like a Scottish loch or a Norwegian fjord, with the wind whipping up the surface angrily, and then it can seem like a mirror, reflecting the blue sky, still and peaceful.

This, then, was the place and the people which awaited the return of Donald Campbell and his *Bluebird.* This, their lake, was to be the arena for a great new joust with the unknown.

Donald stood, before preparing to leave for the north, at the bottom of his garden at Leatherhead. He gazed moodily at the river, lazing along at his feet. Stooping, he picked up a twig and threw it into the still water.

"A ripple like that could cause disaster," he said.

He was speaking to a news reporter who had come down to Surrey to discuss the forthcoming project

"It's the pre-match nerves which always get me – a time when everything is under control, but nothing is ready."

They stood for several minutes as Donald paused to give himself 'a mental trial run on the River Mole, before the trial runs on Coniston later'.

He turned, and led the way back to the house, to get ready for his journey. To follow *Bluebird*, who was already on her way, somewhere on the M6 motorway.

She travelled, swathed in blue plastic sheeting, on a vehicle belonging to Adams Brothers, of New Malden, who were always entrusted with her transport. She caused no trouble to the driver until, having left the A6 at Levens Bridge, she reached the village of Greenodd where her width and the narrowness of the roads began to cause him some embarrassment. Superintendent John Abbott, of the Lancashire Police, gave her an escort of police Land Rovers for the remainder of her journey. Through Torver hamlet, on to Coniston, through the village and over the hump back bridge, past the old church and over the second bridge spanning Church Beck. So to the gate, guarding a rough track over the fields which led down to the lake. *Bluebird* was slowly inched through the gate and on to the track; the driver could not negotiate a tree leaning over the track and took to the field. And there *Bluebird* stayed for the rest of the day, well and truly stuck in the mud.

As though reluctant to face the lake again, as though she sensed what was to come, for a long time she resisted all efforts to move her. Local tractors failed and heavy moving gear had to be called in before she was again brought on to the track and her journey to the boat-house was completed.

A beautiful old craft, the *Gondola*, used to ply her trade on Coniston Water. She was moored at the hundred year-old jetty which juts out into the water at the northerly end of the lake. Alongside the jetty is a steel-railed slipway, on which the *Gondola* was berthed during the winter, and it was on this same slipway that the jet powered *Bluebird*, resting on a specially built wheeled cradle, was berthed.

Above the slipway, tubular steel scaffolding formed a framework, which was sheathed in blue sheeting. This was *Bluebird's* boathouse. Behind this structure, in a double garage, the team assembled a workshop. The site, the garage and the converted boathouse in which he and his family live, belong to Arthur Wilson. Arthur rented the site to the project, and he was to see his 'back garden' badly cut up by traffic before he said goodbye to his winter visitors.

My interest in the project was a natural and obvious one. Not only had I been most impressed with Donald when I was first introduced to him, but I now lived in the Lake District, only some eight miles from Coniston; having missed all previous record attempts I was determined not to miss this one. I was also asked by our local magazine editor to contribute a story in due course. So, together with Paul Allonby, friend and local photographer, I went along to Coniston. We knew the set was being prepared, and we went to see the actors assemble; to look at Coniston Water, not as a lake catering for rowing boat enthusiasts and fishermen, but as the place where a man with a jet-propelled boat hoped to travel at 300 mph.

As we drove to Coniston that first day, Paul told me that the *Daily Sketch* had decided to sponsor this new bid, and he passed me a copy of that day's issue.

'No one has been in the spray-blurred world of 300 mph [it read] .... And we believe Campbell has the will and the guts to find out what might happen, if *Bluebird's* speedometer clicks up over the present record.'

So Donald had at least one backer; he was not alone.

Out of what looked like utter chaos during the first few days, came some semblance of order. One of the Land Rovers which had accompanied the team to Australia was parked at the end of the slipway, its winch to be used for the launching and recovery of *Bluebird*. It was very expensively equipped with meters, gauges and compressors. A caravan – a 'Bluebird' of course – loaned to the project by Border Caravans Limited, stood near the boathouse. This served as office, coffee-house and briefing-room. Two telephones were installed in it, one for Donald,

Arriving at Coniston in 1966 on an Adams Brothers low-loader *(Paul Allonby)*

the other for the press. There was none of the slick organisation which I understood had been a feature of earlier attempts.

No wealthy oil companies were sponsoring this venture so there was no line of telephone booths for the press, no white-coated attendants and no provision for the calls of nature. The grass behind the caravan will be green and flourishing in the spring.

Superintendent Abbott detailed PC Jim to look after security on the site, and he was joined by 'Bill' Jordan of the RAC. Bill's magnificent Dali-esque moustaches – his antennae as we called them – were to be blamed for causing 'static' on the radio-telephone link-up; he challenged all who came to the site, demanding to see their press passes or other identification, and very few of those without good reason for being there got past him.

The Army were called in to advise on communications and eventually they sent a signals party to look after the intercom system – between *Bluebird* and base, and *Bluebird* and support craft.

This then was the stage and, in the absence of the principal actor, who had not yet arrived, Paul and I had a good look at the supporting cast.

Leo Villa of course was there. Bustling, cheerful, genial always busy. He was now sixty-seven, and looked as fit as a fiddle. The man who had said to Donald, several years ago:

"I'm with you, boy – through thick and thin."

Second-in-command to Leo was Maurice Parfitt, smiling, pipe-smoking technical engineer, who had joined the Campbell team in 1954. Donald had tried to dissuade him, explaining that the pay was poor, that the work was hard and the hours long. But Maurice was not to be dissuaded.

Assisting the two engineers were Louis Goosens, Donald's butler, who seemed able to turn his hand to any job, and young Clive Glynn, an apprentice, 'borrowed' from his father's garage with a promise from Donald that he would only be away from home for some two or three weeks. Poor Clive was not to see his home for much longer than that. I am sure he was convinced that crocodiles existed in Coniston Water; someone, in the first few days, assured him of their presence and, whenever he had a free moment during the project, he would be seen gazing at the shallows and banks of the lake, never quite certain that he had not been 'kidded'.

Medical help, if needed, was to be supplied by Stephen Darbishire, a local doctor friend of Donald and a man in whom he placed a good deal of faith. Dr Darbishire helped to man one of the support boats whenever *Bluebird* was out on the lake.

These boats consisted of two Fairline 19's loaned to the project by Oundle Marina; a hired cruiser which the BBC shared with the CBC; a fast, unsinkable dory; and *Jet-Star*, a ski-boat developed by Donald and Leo Villa, powered by a turbo water-jet engine. I was told they hoped to enter this in the 1967 Boat Show with a view to marketing it.

Amongst the many who came to Coniston to watch and report this new attempt were David Benson and Norman Luck of the *Daily Express*, Brian Boss of the *Sketch* and Keith Harrison of the Press Association. Keith was also secretary of the K7 Club, which took its name from *Bluebird's* racing number and whose members are timing officials and pressmen. Geoffrey Hallawell, who had followed all Donald's record attempts and become established as project photographer, was there, and Harry

Bluebird being launched onto Coniston on 4th November 1966.
Tonia Campbell can be seen above the front tip of the port sponson.
The building was the old HQ of the *Gondola* pleasure boat *(Paul Allonby)*

Griffin, although insisting that these record attempts were a damned nuisance and a waste of time, came along. Harry was with the *Lancashire Evening Post* and is also the author of some beautifully written books on the Lake District.

The BBC sent Gerald Harrison, of the *Look North* programme, with a camera crew, and Paul Davies of CBC flew over to make a colour film for Canadian viewers. The independent television companies also sent crews to Coniston.

Many more were to come to the boathouse as the days lengthened into weeks, and as the interest in the project quickened.

Paul and I were talking to Maurice and Louis in the workshop when Maurice, pointing through the window, said:

"Skipper's here."

He was to say this many, many times as the weeks went by.

We looked down the track to see a blue E-type Jaguar, followed by a red Fiat sports saloon approaching. They entered

Donald was christened Noddy at this stage (*Paul Allonby*)

the yard and pulled up alongside the caravan. Donald stepped out of the E-type and threw a quick glance around the crowd gathered to watch him. He wore a dark blue car-coat over a suit of pale blue racing overalls. On his head was a sloppy woollen blue ski-cap, pulled well down over his ears.

He had changed over the years since I had first met him. His face was finer drawn; leaner, and his hair had receded slightly. There was a firmer set to his mouth and a determination about his stride. Obviously, the passage of time and his many experiences – particularly his car crash – had made their mark on him.

With his arrival the whole atmosphere changed. I had heard of his uncanny knack of imposing his will and personality on others, and I was to see it demonstrated now. One felt suddenly, that the project was under way.

From the other car stepped Tonia, Donald's wife, vivacious Belgian-born cabaret star, and with her came glamour to the scene. She chuckled and laughed and greeted old friends, and the serious business of record-breaking became, just for a while, a bit of fun. She wore a black silk trouser suit, and over this a black, plastic, 'Carnaby Street' jacket.

We were to see Tonia many times during the early weeks.

Donald walked straight over to the boathouse and, leaning against one of *Bluebird's* sponsons, became involved in a discussion with a signals officer about the best method of installing a radio-telephone set in the cockpit. Within seconds, the boathouse became a seething mass of photographers, and flash-bulbs popped by the dozen.

It was quite obvious that any apathy with which the announcement of his new bid had been received had now gone. If Donald Campbell was going to get a new record, then he was also going to get his publicity.

That day ended on a hilarious note. The wooden planking of the old jetty, which was moss-covered, had become extremely slippery from recent rain-fall, and we had learned to walk with caution during the day. One somewhat pompous individual, however, not knowing of this hazard and anxious to secure a photograph from the end of the jetty, ran down its full length, found that his braking system was inadequate and plunged gracefully over the edge. Although we recovered him and took him into the village to dry off, I am afraid we laughed.

8

Gremlins

DONALD'S headquarters were at the Sun Hotel, a lovely little pub, old and mellowed, situated in an elevated position above the village where the track leading to the summit of the Old Man begins. The bar in the summer months copes with the thirsts of the many who, carrying heavy rucksacks, and wearing nailed boots, must pass its door when making for or leaving, the fell tops. Its uneven stone floor is scarred with the marks of 'tricounis' and hob nails. Ken, the amiable barman, has seen them all come and go: youngsters, experiencing their first taste of fell-walking and crag-climbing; toughened, weather-beaten cragsmen, who know the classification of every rockface in the district – Moderate, Very Difficult, or Severe; men like John Hunt and Vivian Fuchs who came to practise their rock-craft on Dow Crags; schoolteachers, bringing their families to the Lake District for the umpteenth time; and artists, good and bad, with their folding easels.

And Donald Campbell. For this is Connie Robinson's hotel and these two were great friends. Writing in his book *Into the Water Barrier* of an earlier visit to Coniston, Donald had said:

"I was happy, though a little nostalgic, to be back at Coniston again, and to meet once more Connie Robinson and her husband ... they could never do too much to help us."

This was in the days when the Robinsons kept the Black Bull; when they left to take over the Sun, Donald followed.

He rented Connie's modern bungalow, a few yards from the hotel and took with him Louis Goosens and his wife to look after the domestic affairs – at Donald's Leatherhead home in Surrey, they were his butler and housekeeper.

Leo, Maurice and Clive moved into the hotel, as did many of the pressmen, and those who could not be accommodated overflowed into the Crown, in the village. When every room in the Crown was booked, then the boarding houses opened their doors again and enjoyed an unexpected extension to their season

The Lakeland snack bar opened up again, becoming a venue for the press; eggs, bacon and coffee, at any time of the day, became an established ritual.

Extra supplies of beer, provisions, newspapers and petrol continually poured into the village. I spoke to Eric Simpson, manager of a local brewery one morning, and he told me:

"Do you know, my man at the Crown didn't get to bed until four o'clock this morning. Those press blighters just wouldn't go to bed. He took over a hundred and fifty pounds in the bar before closing time."

From the windows of the bungalow, Donald was able to study the surface conditions of the lake, half a mile away, through his binoculars. On the morning of November 4th, he must have liked what he saw.

The E-type drew up in the yard by the boathouse and Donald stepped out, the woollen bobble on his cap nodding as he walked. He sought out Leo.

"Get her filled up, Unc," he called, "We'll take her out."

There was a stir of excitement in the yard. We all looked at each other and grinned. We were going to see *Bluebird* in action, only two days after her arrival.

Donald noticed the excitement and, frowning slightly, came up to a group of us.

"Now look, boys, this isn't going to be a run. Just a slow beat around off the jetty, to get the feel of her again."

Maurice, perched on *Bluebird's* port sponson, held a length of clear plastic tubing, which led to a large drum of aviation paraffin outside the boathouse. Clive wielded a pump, inserted in the top of the drum, and the fuel flowed into the tank. (This proved to be a very slow, laborious process and in fact the system was later to be changed in favour of an electric pump.)

Donald, fuelling completed, climbed up into the cockpit and called out:

"Right, take the cover off the tail pipe."

Clive unfastened the small clamps which secured a metal 'lid' to the end of the jet-pipe and removed it. Donald gave a thumbs-up signal to Louis, who was sitting at the winch control in the Land Rover. Slowly, very slowly, *Bluebird* on her wheeled

Preparing for a run – the dory towing her from the jetty. The modified water baffles have now been fitted *(Paul Allonby)*

cradle began to move down towards the water. When she floated, free of her cradle, a line was connected to her stern and that of the dory, and she was towed out into deeper water.

When the dory had manoeuvred her so that her nose faced the centre of the lake, the line was cast off and we could see her, sooner than we had expected, afloat, in her own element. And she looked beautiful, purposeful, a machine built to do a job. Although she sat very low in the water, somehow whale-like, one could immediately visualise her at speed, streaking along the surface like a bullet.

Donald pressed the starter button, compressed air hissed, and, within seconds, we heard the familiar whine of a jet engine. Immediately, the boat began to inch forward; as Donald increased power slightly, she gained speed. Vapour issued from

Preparing for a run, with *Jet-Star* in the background.
Note the inadvertently inverted Union Jack *(Paul Allonby)*

her jet-pipe, the water at her stern became turbulent, and Donald taxied her around the bay at perhaps 10 to 12 miles an hour. Testing the feel of her, testing her steering, and familiarising himself once more with her controls.

Ten minutes later he brought her back. When she was alongside the jetty, he crawled along her engine cowling and stepped down on to the narrow fin at her stern. He took the end of a boat-hook held by Maurice on the jetty; *Bluebird* was aligned on her cradle and winched slowly back under cover. For the first time since she captured her existing record of 276.33 mph in Australia, *Bluebird* and her pilot had been together again afloat.

Donald expressed himself as very satisfied with the test and, before leaving, advised us all that there would be a static engine test the following day. We left that evening feeling that all was well. We had seen *Bluebird* in action, albeit slowly. The launch-

Winching *Bluebird* in after a run *(Paul Allonby)*

ing and recovery system had proved satisfactory. And we were promised a demonstration of the sting in her tail the following day. Given the weather we felt Donald would have his record very soon now.

Bluebird's 'power-pack' this time was a Bristol-Siddeley 'Orpheus' jet engine. In their quest for speeds around the 300 mph mark, Donald, Ken Norris and the team had chosen the Orpheus as the engine most likely to give them the result they wanted. It was the engine used by the RAF in their Gnat fighters and it pushed these aircraft through the skies at some 600 mph. Its thrust was 5,000 pounds and it consumed 600 gallons of aviation paraffin per hour. The old engine used in Australia had been removed, *Bluebird* had been modified and adapted, and the Orpheus – on loan to the project from the Air Ministry – had been installed.

We learnt something of the power of this engine on November 5th. A schoolteacher enjoying a winter holiday in his caravan at

Coniston had earlier offered Donald his services should any skin-diving be required during the project. Before the static test, he donned his rubber diving suit and, entering the water which covered the slipway, he shackled *Bluebird's* stern to the steel rails with heavy cables and chains. With the Land Rover winch cable holding her at the forward end she was held secure, immobilised. Everything left lying loose in the boathouse was picked up and stowed away so that nothing could be sucked into the air intakes. The tail-pipe cover was removed and Donald stepped up into the cockpit.

He pressed the starter, releasing compressed air, and the engine rotated. Air was thus drawn into the combustion chambers, vaporised fuel was mixed with it and, in seconds, the mixture was 'lit' by an electric spark. The engine began to whine, at an ever increasing pitch, until finally Donald gave the throttle 'full bore'.

We stood, hands to our ears, watching the tremendous jet-streams issuing from the tail-pipe; watching the water being lashed into a frenzy of spray and spume. A hat flew from the head of one who stood too close to the fury. And then – when Donald's foot on the throttle must have been touching the floor – came 'expensive noises'. The roar and the whine died down, the engine stopped on a grinding, metallic note, and Donald's face registered dismay.

"What the hell? What the devil's happened?"

Subsequent and prolonged investigation showed that the air intakes, originally designed, and found successful, for the old, less powerful engine, had proved inadequate for the demands of the Orpheus. This engine consumed two tons of air per minute and the air intakes had succumbed. They collapsed; loosened rivets were sucked through into the engine and the turbine blades were wrecked.

Donald's face that day registered a mixture of emotions: anger and bewilderment. And when it was finally realised that the engine was a complete 'write off' he walked to his car, slammed the door and was away.

The question on everyone's lips was: "Why had this fault only come to light now? Could there not have been a static engine test before *Bluebird* was sent up to Coniston? What had the boffins been doing?"

No one supplied the answer and work commenced on the removal of the damaged intakes – work which was to last well into the night. The following morning we said goodbye to Donald, as he left for London. Paul Allonby strolled up, packing his camera away in his 'gadget box.'

"Well, come along Arthur. That's the end of the project."

But it wasn't. Donald and Leo had other ideas. The telephone at the Sun had been put to much use and Donald was not on his way back home, but was taking the air intakes for strengthening and modification; he was back again six days later.

In the meantime, a huge mobile crane arrived at the boathouse, and was positioned alongside *Bluebird*. Leo and his team worked round the clock at the task of removing the damaged engine. Specially made clamps and brackets were bolted to the engine, these in turn being bolted to a carrying rig. The hook of the crane was placed in the 'eye' of the rig, and the engine was lifted out.

Decisions had obviously been made. Leo knew exactly what he was doing. A new engine would be found for *Bluebird*, but the old engine was to be patched up and put into running order again, in order that the intakes – when they returned – could be given a test. The team was kept busy throughout that week, repairing and re-installing the engine.

Donald, in order to acquire another Orpheus engine, had to purchase a 'used' Gnat aircraft complete. We heard that he paid £10 over the scrap price for the aircraft, but the actual sum was not disclosed. The engine, accompanied by Bristol-Siddeley technicians, arrived at Coniston, and on November 11th it was completely dismantled and cleaned.

The weather chose to be very unkind whilst all this work was going on. Gale force winds, accompanied by heavy rain, combined to make life a misery. The boathouse, a mere temporary structure of scaffolding and plastic sheeting, buckled and strained in the wind and very nearly collapsed. Louis and Clive spent almost two days perched on the flimsy roof, baling water and lashing guy ropes.

That the Plastolene sheeting was not torn into shreds by the force of the wind, but remained, strong, firm and intact, was a splendid testimonial to its quality. The clear sheet in the roof, which permitted light to enter the boat-house, was estimated to be holding a thousand gallons of rainwater at one stage.

On November 6th, the blue E-type pulled into the yard. Donald was back. He brought with him the modified intakes, having crammed three weeks' work into one, and that evening they were installed, and given a static test with the old engine. They proved successful and the bar at the Sun was full that night. The project was alive again.

Two days of very hard work followed. The old engine was hoisted out of the boat and was placed on the ground outside the workshop. There it remained, in all weathers, for six weeks. The damaged turbine blades could be seen and were examined by all who came to the boathouse.

The new engine was installed under the supervision of the Bristol-Siddeley engineers and on the 18th, with Coniston Water looking like a sheet of glass, Donald announced that he was taking *Bluebird* out. Immediately there was excitement and activity again. It had been two weeks since we had last seen the boat on the water. There had been a fear that the project had come to an end when the engine was damaged; now it seemed that perhaps we should see *Bluebird* in a high-speed run after all. The Coniston grapevine got to work. All the press and the photographers, all the TV camera crews, and all those who could get past the man at the gate, came rushing down to the boathouse. The yard, the track and the fields alongside were filled with cars. Some of the photographers drove around the eastern side of the lake to the points where the official timekeepers would be during record attempts. They hoped to secure their first shots of *Bluebird* at speed. They were to be disappointed.

The same routine we had seen on November 4th, was used again. The tail-pipe cover was removed, the winch was started, and *Bluebird* took to the water. This time the dory did not tow her out into the lake. She was aligned at an angle off the end of the jetty and we saw Donald put on his face mask – which carried the radio-telephone mike – his tiny life-jacket and a leather helmet. I also saw Mr Whoppit for the first time.

Mr Whoppit is a small teddy-bear, presented to Donald some years ago by his manager, Peter Barker. And Donald, whether driving *Bluebird* the car, or *Bluebird* the boat, would not move off if Mr Whoppit was not in the cockpit with him. This was his own mascot together with his father's mascot, which was fitted to the dashboard of every one of Donald's cars or boats. The latter was a metal plate etched with a drawing of a bird and bearing the words *The Blue Bird*. Alongside this was a Saint Christopher medallion, so made that it hinged open to reveal the signatures of Donald's team, who had presented it to him

Donald started the engine at the jetty and gently, slowly, the boat commenced to move away. He drew the perspex cockpit canopy over his head and locked it. Increasing power slightly, when he was sure the boat was clear of the jetty, he taxied out to the centre of the lake.

Many of us dashed around to the beach which affords a full view of the length of Coniston Water, and a TV camera crew set up their tripod on the roof of a Ford Zodiac, the sound engineer holding up his barrel-mike to capture the noise of the 'take-off'.

But there was no take-off. Donald pointed *Bluebird's* nose down the lake and 'gave her the gun'. She moved forward, at perhaps 30 to 40 miles per hour. Huge mounds of water poured over her sponsons, clouds of spray created by the jet-stream streamed out behind her, and we waited for her to lift into planing position; for her sponsons to rise to the surface and her stern to 'unstick' before hurtling along at high speed.

But *Bluebird* wasn't having any. She wallowed, she dipped her nose, and for a moment we lost sight of her in the spray. Four times Donald tried to bring her up on to her planing points and then, finally, he motored back to the jetty.

'The water's putting the bloody fire out, Unc," he called to Leo, who stood looking thoughtful on the jetty.

"Bring her in, Skipper. Bring her in."

Donald looked worried and as *Bluebird* was winched up the slipway he ignored the questions thrown at him by pressmen on the jetty. He left the cockpit and the team went into a huddle in the boathouse.

Once the fault was recognised, Leo and the team went to work at once to kick yet another gremlin out of the Coniston base. *Bluebird* had been fitted with two perspex guards, curved to conform to the shape of the air intakes, one at the side of each intake. They were designed to deflect the water thrown up by the sponsons when the boat was moving at slow speeds. They had proved adequate for the earlier, smaller engine, but the Orpheus,

Paul Wyand of Movietone News on a Ford Zodiac, preparing to film the event.
Despite his size, Paul was renowned for his ability to pan a camera smoothly for
high-speed action photographic events. *(Paul Allonby)*

with its greater thrust, was forcing the sponsons down into the water, causing great quantities of water to enter the air intakes and thus 'putting the fire out'.

It became obvious to us that one could not just bring a boat along to Coniston and crack a record with it. Not just like that. It was a game of trial and error, requiring much patience, from Donald, from his team and from the onlookers. And not all the snags which developed could be hidden. There was no privacy. They all worked in the full glare of publicity. Nor was there any means whereby Donald could explain to the crowds standing around the shores of Coniston Water why – with the lake as smooth as a mirror – *Bluebird* was not streaking along the measured kilometre. Those of us privileged to be at the boathouse felt a great deal of sympathy for him.

The water guards were re-designed and modified many times. Perspex of half-inch thickness was obtained from Vickers' shipyard at Barrow, and many experiments were made before the guards were declared satisfactory. One more week went by, which brought us to November 22nd, and on that morning Donald decided that *Bluebird* should be given another trial.

Once again, the news spread quickly and the cars bumped their way down the track to the boathouse. Once more the cameras were set up and vantage points were sought. Perhaps now, with the boat fitted with her new water guards – looking like wings on each side of the cockpit – we should see her at speed.

But the gremlins had not yet finished their mischief. There was to be more hard work for Leo and the boys.

Donald took *Bluebird* slowly into the centre of the lake and, lining her up, applied the power to the engine. As the boat gathered speed, it was obvious to us that less water was being thrown up into the air intakes, that the perspex guards were now doing their job. The engine continued to run and Donald applied more throttle. Surely, now she would rise to her planing points? But no – after four short runs she was back at the slipway and being winched up into the boathouse.

There was much muttering. Small groups formed and we all began to ask what the hell had gone wrong now. Why hadn't Donald, with such perfect surface conditions, given us all a demonstration of what the boat could do? Even 100 mph would have satisfied us. Was he trying to drag this business out for some reason of his own?

Jim Sherdley gave me a nudge.

"What do you suppose they are doing now?" he asked, pointing to where Bill Jordan and young Clive were busy filling two sandbags from a pile near the caravan.

"Search me," I said. "Perhaps they are potting plants in the boathouse."

But the spirit of Heath Robinson must have walked around the lake that day and dropped a hint to Leo. For it appears that he had suggested to Donald that they tie a sandbag on each side of *Bluebird's* tail, and that he take her out like that. And that is exactly what they did. Sandbags were lashed on each side of the transom, *Bluebird* was winched back into the water, her engine started and, within seconds of reaching the centre of the lake, she was away. Up she came on to her three planing points and, for the first time since the project started, we saw her doing the job for which she had been designed. Not wallowing deep in the water, but up on the surface, travelling at speed. It was not very

"Up she came on to her three planing points and, for the first time since the project started, we saw her doing the job for which she had been designed." *(Paul Allonby)*

fast. Perhaps a hundred miles per hour. But we were pleased and when Donald brought the boat back to the slipway it was quite obvious that he was pleased too.

Rumour had it that the second Orpheus engine had proved to be some 200 pounds lighter than the first, and that this was the cause of *Bluebird's* nose-heaviness. Leo Villa, however, assured me that this was not so. The two engines were identical in weight, he told me, although they were heavier than the Beryl engine with the smaller amount of thrust, which had previously powered *Bluebird*. The cause of the nose-heaviness was the different location of the Orpheus in the hull. It was all, in fact, a case of trial and error, until the correct balance was found.

Norman Buckley, visiting the site to watch the trial runs, sent his man off to the boat-yards in Bowness Bay. When he returned, driving Norman's Lotus Elan, it looked very low down on its suspension. He opened the boot to reveal a quantity of lead ingots, which we all helped to carry into the boathouse. Louis and Bill Jordan, meanwhile, had been visiting builders' yards, and returned loaded with sheets of roofing lead.

Working very late into the night, the team melted the lead down and made castings the thickness of a telephone directory, which were bolted into the hull, beneath the engine at the stern.

Before he left the base that day, to return to the Sun, Donald promised us:

"Two hundred and fifty miles per hour by the weekend."

However, although he took *Bluebird* out on the following morning and completed five runs, his top speed was only 120 mph. *Bluebird* struck a drifting log and sustained slight damage.

Then the weather intervened. High winds and driving rain returned to Coniston; the lake looked like the sea off the Cornish coast during a storm, and the Old Man was blotted from sight by low-lying cloud.

So November passed and the project was one month old. On December 2nd, Donald complained of back pains from an old injury and left with Tonia for London to visit an osteopath.

9

"Skipper's here"

DURING Donald's absence from Coniston we all continued to visit the boathouse each day, for the project was now very much alive and full of interest. I tried to make comparisons between this and other projects, but it was no use – this record-breaking business was something quite unique and there was nothing with which to compare it. It was all so unlike anything in my previous experience. Some of those who shared the sixty-four days of Coniston with Donald Campbell had seen if all before. Certainly Harry Griffin had. He claimed to have witnessed all Donald's record-breaking ventures in this country and, indeed, told us that he had once accompanied Donald on a run, in the days of the *Bluebird* with the double cockpit.

"Leo wanted to study the boat's performance," he told us. "So Donald asked me to accompany him. We had a run at a hundred and forty miles per hour."

Geoffrey Hallawell, the freelance photographer from Manchester whom Donald described as an ex-officio member of his team, had seen it all before. Once, at Coniston, Donald had driven *Bluebird* past a press launch, clearing it by nine feet. The occupants had repeatedly asked for a close-up shot of the boat at speed. However, when they were given their opportunity, they were so petrified with fear that one of them jumped overboard and only Geoff got his picture.

Certainly Norman Buckley was no stranger to this game: he was a great friend of Donald and indeed had competed against him at one time, on Lake Garda. He, as official observer, had seen it all many times. And the second observer, Andrew Brown, Kendal business man – 'dear old Andy' as Donald called him – had been with the team at Ullswater and at Lake Mead.

To Leo Villa and Maurice Parfitt, and to Ken Norris, the whole thing was a way of life. They were a major part of the whole record-breaking set-up, and Leo had seen two generations of it.

Donald with his friend Norman Buckley, who was one of the official observers *(David Watt)*

There was no lack of old hands then. But to me, and to many of the others who gathered at Coniston in November 1966, it was something completely new.

I have played in minor, and witnessed many major, golf tournaments where a bunch of men fight a battle to see who comes out on top. I have seen test matches played at Leeds and the Oval, and watched the big names duelling at Silverstone and Oulton Park. But the project at Coniston was like none of these. There was no competition, no opposition: only Donald's fear of what the Americans were up to – and many thought this was a nebulous fear.

However, as the days stretched out into weeks, and November came to an end, the project came to hold a strange fascination for us all and Coniston became for us, too, a way of life.

The day would start for me with a drive over from Windermere; past the River Brathay; past the Drunken Duck inn; skirting Tarn Hows; and on, over the fell roads to Hawkshead Hill. When the hair-pin bend was reached, on the drop down to the village, I could see the whole length of Coniston Water, as though seen from an aircraft. The whole arena was there, laid out in front of me. The broad, northern end, where the lights of the blue boathouse twinkled in the early morning mist; the long central stretch where the measured kilometre had been marked out; and the tapering southern reach, with its dog-leg and little island.

It was at this view-point that Donald, leaving Coniston after an unsuccessful earlier mission, had stopped his car to have a last look at the lake, and had said:

"You bitch! But we'll be back."

If I had received an early morning call from Bill Jordan, which meant that conditions seemed favourable for *Bluebird,* then I would know that I would be looking down at a glass-like surface when I reached the view-point and that I would probably see the support boats setting out on their task of 'sweeping' the lake, picking up tree branches and debris from the surface.

All too often, though, I was to see the lake in angry mood, with its surface cut up into waves by the strong winds and with its surrounding fells shrouded in low cloud. And over the weeks it was to seem that, when conditions were right, *Bluebird* was not ready, some snag had developed; and when *Bluebird* and Donald were fit and anxious to go, the conditions were too bad.

Arrival at the boathouse usually meant a greeting from Bill Jordan or one of the pressmen, who would lean out of the caravan doorway and call: "Coffee?" And the day would start, sitting reading the newspapers and sipping hot coffee made with evaporated milk. We would read the short paragraphs sent by the reporters to their editors the night before and which nearly always seemed to say:

"Donald Campbell, seeking his new world water speed record was unable to take *Bluebird* out today, due to unfavourable weather."

The next move in the day would be the arrival of Leo and Maurice in a Vauxhall car loaned to the project by Arthur Chapman of Ulverston. Louis and Clive would follow in a Morris brake. The compressor would be started, the lighting in the workshop and the boathouse would come on and Clive would switch on the space heater in the boathouse. If it was a day of turned-up coat collars and stamping feet, there would be a rush to the space heater and soon the boathouse would be crowded. That Leo never lost his patience and kicked us all out was indeed a blessing, as this was the only warm spot on the site. He would merely give us a "good morning" and a quizzical look, and get on with the job in hand. Leo gained the affection and respect of everyone there.

One morning, as Leo busied himself at the bench in the workshop, I called to him:

"Leo – quietly – just come here a minute."

I pointed to a many-coloured chaffinch which, perched on the wing of a car, was busy pecking away at its own reflection in the wing mirror. Leo was charmed and went for his camera. By the time he returned another photographer had spotted the bird and was busy focusing on it. There was no room for the two of them and Leo failed to get his picture. In spite of all the snags he encountered during the project, and all the hard work he put into it, this was the only occasion when I saw him annoyed.

When Campbell was at Coniston, the highlight of each day would be the arrival of the E-type Jaguar.

There would be the familiar call of "Skipper's here" from one of the team, and we would all turn to watch the car, bumping its way along the rough track, ploughing through the muddy puddles until, reaching the yard, Donald would park it and step out.

The mood of the morning would be written on his face. If angry or worried, his greeting would be curt. He would stalk off to the workshop and become involved with some job. If the mood was good, he would hail us with "good morning, gentlemen", and pause to chat with us.

One morning he arrived and could not find room to park his car. He strode over to me and said:

"Arthur – move your car, will you? And get the other bloody cars sorted out. Team by the caravan, boat crews in the yard, and the press in the woods. Where the hell's Bill? It's his job."

On another occasion, during a television interview, Gerald Harrison asked him – referring to the damaged engine – if he did not think that it had been a mistake to run the static test at full power. Donald almost 'blew his top'.

"No, it jolly well was not a mistake," he stormed. "How else could we test it?"

But the bad moods were rare. More often than not he was cheerful, friendly, darting about between boathouse and

workshop, dealing with reporters, giving television interviews –
and smoking incessant cigars.

His expressions were those of the P. G. Wodehouse days. He
would call us 'old boy', 'old sport' or 'old fruit', and he loved his
own jokes. Once, having told me a hoary old one about the
bishop and the actress, he walked away, laughing uproariously,
glancing back to make quite sure I had taken the point.

During the preparations for one television interview, the
director was posing his cast, telling Leo to 'pop up there',
Maurice to 'pop up here', and Donald, watching this, said
quietly:

"And I suppose I pop off, do I?"

He was a consummate actor. His voice when he was being
interviewed deepened and he spoke with authority. During the
making of a film by one of the independent television companies, he was posed sitting in *Bluebird's* cockpit, facing camera
and microphone; he told again, very quietly and sincerely, the
story of his 'vision'. During his record-breaking attempt with the
car on Lake Eyre he had had a nerve-racking first run.

"I damned nearly killed myself and I knew the second run
would probably be worse. I sat back in the cockpit, looking up at
the opened canopy. And there, reflected in it, I saw my father's
face quite clearly. For a few seconds he looked at me and then
said: 'Well, boy, now you know how I felt that time at Utah. But
don't worry, it'll be all right, boy.'

"Then he faded away. Explain it as you will – I cannot. But it
happened."

I had heard it before. I had read it before. But, listening to him
repeating the story there at Coniston, we were impressed.

As he sat there in the cockpit, he complained of the cold and
suggested that they all adjourn for a brandy. Turning to an attractive continuity girl standing in the boathouse, the sound
engineer said:

"Go and fetch Donald some brandy, Annabel," and then
turning back to Donald, he said:

"Or would you rather have Annabel?"

There was a chuckle from the back of the boathouse and a
voice murmured:

"If I know Donald, he'll choose Annabel."

Laughing, we turned to find Tonia standing in the entrance. It was lunchtime, and she had come to collect her husband.

The various television companies kept him busy. Alan Weekes, of the BBC *Sportsview* programme, came along with a crew of cameramen, sound engineers and a producer, and filmed a long interview with him which we all watched the following evening. Another team filmed him standing under a huge golf umbrella on the jetty, looking pensively at the rain-lashed surface of the lake. For yet another team, he took them out on the lake in *Jet-Star* and there he patiently submitted to a very long interview, drifting with the boat's engine stopped.

We were very interested to watch the 'tricks of the trade' being used during these television interviews, the techniques which are applied before we see the finished product on the home screen. One example was the use of 'cut-ins' as I was told they are called. The interviewer would 'feed' Donald with quite lengthy questions, to draw him out, put him at his ease and ensure a detailed reply. When however, the filming was ended, the interviewer would again pose before the camera and repeat the questions, but this time in a much shorter, more condensed form; these would be the questions that we heard when the film was seen. Donald no doubt had seen it all before but he stood watching the cut-in sequence with tongue in cheek.

"More to this business than meets the eye" he said.

He was a patient man. One morning a small bus bumped into the yard and from it stepped perhaps twenty or thirty schoolboys, accompanied by a master. Obviously this was a pre-arranged visit, for Donald greeted them immediately and took them to see the old engine lying outside the workshop. He knelt down and pointed to the damaged turbine blades, explaining to them exactly what had happened.

Then, leading them into the boathouse, he allowed them to have a good look at *Bluebird* before, grouping them together, he leaned against a sponson, lit a small cigar, and said:

"Now, boys – any questions? Fire away."

They peppered him with questions; they came at him thick and fast. What happened when he pressed *Bluebird's* starter. Why was compressed air used to start the engine? How long was she? How wide was she? And he answered them all. Finally, one small boy asked him:

Donald at the controls of K7 *(photo supplied by Ray Hewartson)*

"What does it feel like, sir, travelling in a boat at three hundred miles per hour?"

He smiled, and quietly replied:

"I don't know, old boy – not yet."

Before they left, each boy produced a sheet of school exercise paper and he autographed every one.

Tonia was with Donald during the first few weeks at Coniston and she added the necessary touch of glamour to the drab scene whenever she came to the boathouse. One could sense that Donald was pleased to have her there. She sparkled and bubbled.

During her stay she had a booking to sing in cabaret in Carlisle, but she found rehearsal in the bungalow difficult; she hired the village hall for a pound, and, shivering in the cold, she practised her numbers there. Before leaving for Carlisle, she came down to the boathouse to say goodbye to Donald. As she left in her little sports car, he said:

"Remember, darling – no driving home by yourself in the dark."

Gerald Harrison interviewed her in the bungalow for the *Look North* programme, and she described her life as the wife of a record-breaker:

"I know the danger he is in, all the time. But it is something he has to do, so I go along with him. He is a big man you know – out of his time maybe – but he is a big man."

I watched Tonia one morning as she stood on the old jetty. A girl from the village, knowing her from an earlier visit, came up to her carrying a baby. She placed the child in Tonia's arms and for a long time Tonia stood there with eyes for nothing else. Donald, and *Bluebird*, and the project, could have been miles away.

When Donald left for London to receive attention to his back, Tonia went with him and we were not to see her again until January.

So life at Coniston became a routine. Chatting, watching, listening. Eggs and bacon at the snack bar. Beer at the Sun. Coffee in the caravan. Coffee in the workshop – and this was the best coffee of the lot, sent down each morning at eleven o'clock from the hotel, it arrived in large vacuum flasks. One morning, having been sitting in the car reading the paper, I stepped out for a breather. Donald called out:

"Where've you been, old boy? – your coffee's going cold."

So I became one of the eleven o'clock regulars. And the coffee was good; it was laced with brandy.

And friends were made at Coniston, and old friends and colleagues met again. And the gossip went the rounds.

"Did you hear that the *Sketch* bought the second engine for Donald? Paid something like £15,000 I believe."

"No. I heard he had bought it himself. Had to buy a complete Gnat aircraft to get it. Paid £10 over the scrap price."

"Heard about the American offer?"

"No. What's that?"

"If he gets his record before midnight on New Year's Eve, he gets a packet of money from two American firms."

"Oh God! We shall be home before then, shan't we?"

"I expect so. Donald will be keen to get on with it. This lot must be costing a packet."

"Seven hundred a week, I hear."

"Oh – much more than that."

"What a damned silly time of year to choose for a record attempt. Just look at that ruddy lake."

"It can change in an hour up here, you know. You ask the locals."

"It's the still sharp, frosty mornings he wants. When the thermals flatten the lake."

"Now who's getting technical?"

"Well, I'm hanged if I'm coming down here again until I'm sure the boat's going out."

And, after the first few days of keen interest, when Donald Campbell and *Bluebird* had been closely examined, and the initial novelty had worn off, many of the pressmen retired to their hotels; to stay there until the grapevine told them that action was imminent. Then, there would be a surge of cars, splashing down the track towards the boathouse, or speeding along the winding, narrow road along the east bank of the lake to watch events from the timekeepers' positions.

The Longines timekeeping team arrived on the scene very early in November, a Swiss party under the supervision of M. Raoul Crelerot. He was an elderly, balding, genial man and knew no English. Our conversations with him were frequently hilarious but, somehow, we made ourselves understood. He and his boys proved to be patient and long-suffering, spending many bitterly cold hours perched on their tiny wooden platforms with the icy waters of the lake lapping at their feet.

As the days passed by, those who were to man the support boats began to get themselves organised. Keith Harrison, staff reporter with the Press Association, was appointed by universal acclaim, "Commodore" of the small fleet, and soon the two Fairlines were decorated with red 'day-glow' adhesive sheeting, and each bore a long pole carrying inflated plastic spheres, perhaps two feet in diameter. Whenever *Bluebird* was due for a run, these boats were positioned near the timekeepers' stations, immediately opposite the marker buoys at each end of the kilometre. Thus Donald would have a splash of colour on which to sight.

Louis Goosens and Bill Jordan manned the fast dory when on stand-by and they were sent down to the south end of the lake to act as a re-fuelling point. The *Jet-Star* was used by Donald as his personal taxi and it proved to be a very impressive craft, with a speed of between 40 and 50 miles per hour. He took me for a run in her one afternoon and demonstrated her ability to cope with sharp turns at speed, shouting over his shoulder:

"She'll pull six skiers at once, you know."

When I demurred at his suggested selling price of £1,200, he shrugged saying:

"Development of this sort of thing costs a packet. Someone has to pay for it, old boy."

We of the Lake District object very strongly to the commonly accepted fallacy that "it always rains in the Lakes". We do admit, however, that when it does rain, it makes a thorough job of it. We received many examples of this during the month of November. Heavy clouds moving in over the Old Man seemed to choose the Coniston Campbell base as a depository for their contents with depressing frequency. The soft earth around the boathouse became a soggy quagmire and an elevated path had to be made between boathouse and workshop. The large potholes in the track across the fields became pools of mud and the colour of the cars which made the trip regularly became a uniform grey. Wellington boots were an essential part of one's equipment; if you were foolish enough to stray off the track and take your car on to the field, there you stayed until half a dozen helpers came to push you out.

We must have been a stoical lot. But if Donald and Leo and the team were willing to stick it out, then so were we. If, despite the many snags and the appalling weather, this chap was determined to carry on until he had his record, then we would stick around until he got it.

Donald had his other supporters, too. Every day, cars were parked at the boating beach which afforded a view of the boathouse, and they were parked, too, up on the hill on the other side of the lake. At the weekend hundreds of cars came and their occupants waited, and watched – even though they could see that weather conditions were hopeless. People would walk along the beach until they reached Church Beck and they would stand for hours peering across, hoping for a sight of Donald. Whenever

Donald Campbell's hydrojet *Jet-Star (courtesy of the Lakeland Motor Museum)*

they caught a glimpse of him, there would be a staccato rattle of camera shutters being clicked.

On December 3rd, we received news from Leo that Donald was on his way back from London, having been away only a couple of days.

10

"It's Settling, Chaps"

NOVEMBER had done its very best to ruin the project completely. The gales had battered the boathouse, the rains had flooded the fields, and the level of the lake had risen to such an extent that *Bluebird's* transom was almost under water on the sloping slipway. We sloshed around in thick mud and whenever a car entered the yard we would scatter to one side to avoid being splashed. The potholed track began to look like a causeway with the lake waters lapping on either side, and Arthur Wilson assured me that it was quite possible for his house near the jetty to be completely marooned.

It had been a month, however, full of interest. Engineering feats had been performed on *Bluebird* in absurd conditions. This was no fully equipped factory, staffed with many mechanics. There were only a flimsy boathouse and a makeshift workshop, and a mere handful of men.

They were dedicated men, though. Leo, Maurice, Louis and Clive had worked unstintingly, putting in very long hours and getting very little sleep. And Donald had not retired to his bunga-low, letting them get on with it; he had been there, working just as hard as any of them.

So December came in, and with it came a different atmosphere. Donald returned from London on the 4th and we all felt that the project was under way again. We knew *Bluebird* had been declared fit, and we all hoped that Donald's osteopath had succeeded in easing his pain. The clouds had lifted from the summit of the Old Man and the skies were blue over Coniston.

We reckoned without the wind however. Donald needed a flat calm lake, but for six days a cold south easterly wind cut up the surface into a four-inch 'popple'.

The papers again printed their daily 'apologia' explaining that

"*Bluebird* was again confined to her boathouse due to high winds."

Not everyone appreciated Donald's problems. One disgruntled pressman strolled up to me one bitterly cold morning, rubbing his hands to restore circulation.

"One man's damned vanity keeping us here, you know. At one time, I was prepared to believe him when he said he was doing it for Britain. Not now though – he's spinning this out for his own benefit. There's some reason for all this delay."

I pointed at the lake, at the wavelets lapping the shore.

"Don't you suppose that that has something to do with it?"

"Oh – to hell with that. The boat's supposed to ride over the top of that, isn't it?"

Johnnie Manders, a photographer who had been listening to this, asked quietly:

"Would you like to do it instead?"

Our friend ambled away, muttering something about "I'm not paid to do it – he is."

Discussion then started amongst a group of us about the cost of this project. Was Donald footing most of the bill himself? We knew the *Daily Sketch* was sponsoring him; we were constantly reminded of this by the banners which the *Sketch* had draped on the trees near the boathouse. Donald himself had told us all during a television interview that Monty Berman, the theatre impresario, had also chipped in. He had described how, during a luncheon meeting, Monty had said:

"Donald, I'm terribly interested in this project of yours. Would you be very embarrassed if I offered you a thousand pounds?"

"Embarrassed?" Donald replied; "Monty, old boy, you have just bought yourself the new engine installation."

But we knew of no other backers. These were the days of "squeeze" conditions, days of withdrawal, and the big companies who had been ready to help in the old days were not forthcoming this time. It certainly looked as if Donald Campbell was carrying the can.

When a white Alfa Romeo 'Giulia' drew up into the yard one morning and out of it stepped the slim figure of Lady Aitken, we had another thought. Was the *Express* taking an interest now? Was any help coming from that direction?

At about 7 o'clock on Saturday morning, December 10th, my telephone rang, and I reached sleepily for the receiver.

"This is Bill, Arthur. You'd better get over here. Phone Paul, will you? It looks as if there may be a run."

The drive over the fell roads called for some care that morning. Black ice had made the corners hazardous and the journey took a little longer. When I reached the viewpoint, the twilight of dawn was lifting and Coniston Water had a glassy surface. The sky was clear and the Old Man wore a dusting of snow. The icy wind which had been nibbling away at our tempers for the last few days had died away.

I reached the boathouse in time to join a group of pressmen gathered around Donald.

"This is just going to be a steady run, to test the braking system. And we shall need several such runs before we start thinking of any records. *Bluebird* has to be worked up."

Learning that the timekeepers were setting up their equipment down on the other side of the lake, and realising that it would take at least half an hour for the support boats to carry out their sweep of the course before going to their stations, I decided to watch the run from the timekeepers' positions.

I took note of the time it took to drive from the boat-house around the head of the lake and along the narrow tortuous road, past Ruskin's old home, Brantwood, to the northern end of the measured kilometre. I imagined myself speeding back to the boathouse one day in the near future to be in time to congratulate Donald when he got his record.

When I arrived at the stony beach with its small wooden platform built out into the water, the timekeepers had already set up their watches, the two Fairlines had taken up their positions to act as temporary marker buoys, and Norman Buckley, having received a call from Donald early that morning, was standing gazing up the lake towards the boathouse.

Someone called "He's away!" and the small crowd of us watched as away in the distance a plume of spray rose above the lake surface. Within seconds *Bluebird* was up to us, and past us. Riding high on her planing points, her jet engine roaring, she streaked away to the south end of the lake. To me, she looked fast, but the more knowledgeable ones guessed that she had been travelling at only about a hundred and sixty.

Bluebird at the jetty *(Paul Allonby)*

Minutes later, when the wash and the air disturbance of her first run had subsided, Donald brought her back and again she sped past us, trailing a long comet-tail spray.

After Norman Buckley had conferred with the timekeepers and they had checked by telephone with their colleagues at the other end of the kilometre, he was asked what the speeds had been. Noncommittal, he shrugged and, entering his car, set off for the boathouse.

By the time I returned to the base, Donald had *Bluebird* aligned on the cradle which awaited her in the water. He called out to me to throw a rubber dinghy into the water between the hull of the boat and the jetty and, as he climbed out of the cockpit and stepped down towards the dinghy, Harry Griffin shouted questions across to him. Donald slipped and gave his thumb a nasty crack on the Perspex guard. He glared over his shoulder at me as he sucked at the blood which appeared, and said,

"I'll love you for that, old boy!"

Then, as though realising that the fault was not mine, he turned his attention to poor Harry, saying:

"That's through asking your bloody questions at a time like this."

However, when he reached *Bluebird's* stern and stood on the narrow ledge, he grinned and gave us a wink. All was well again.

Stepping down from the boat, and leaving the boathouse, he was at once surrounded by reporters anxious for news of the run; he stood answering their questions for several minutes. I stood with Gerald Harrison watching this, and asked Gerald if he knew what the speeds had been.

"Yes," he replied. "He did a hundred and ninety six miles per hour on the first run, and two hundred and two on the second. On average he just cracked the two hundred."

This had been a good day and it looked as though the long weeks of waiting would soon come to an end. The snags and frustrations were now things of the past, and Donald had just done 200 mph. Let him get on with his brake tests, and with the business of "working *Bluebird* up" – it would not be long now.

The previous day, Donald had explained to a few of us how the braking system worked. The brake fitted to the centre of *Bluebird's* transom was housed in a steel box and consisted simply of a steel rod, a few inches in length and perhaps one and a quarter inches in diameter. This rod was actuated hydraulically, controlled by Donald in the cockpit, and moved up and down in its housing. Only about two inches entered the water during braking, but this was sufficient to check the boat and slow her down from high speeds.

"It must be used very delicately," he told us. "No jamming it on like a car's brakes."

He explained the problem of 'drag' to us. Drag is the resistance of the water when an object passes through it. He suggested we pull a sixpence through water, first at a slow speed and then more quickly.

"It begins to feel like a half-a-crown. And it's the same with this brake. When it hits the water, it's as though it's hitting half-set concrete."

Donald also pointed out the rudder, mounted on the port side of the transom, and the compensating stabilising fin, mounted on the starboard side. He explained that only about three to four

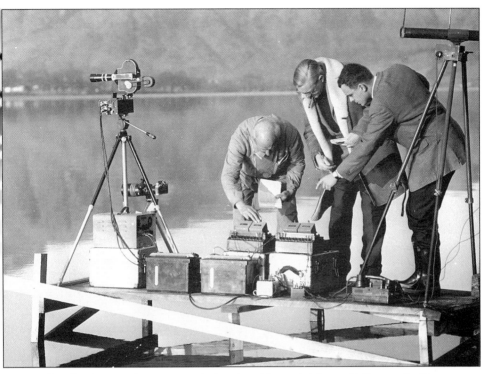

The official timekeepers checking the Longines Chronocinégines, with Norman Buckley in the centre. *(Paul Allonby)*

inches of these two units were in contact with the water at high speed.

We began to feel a new respect for Donald Campbell. This sort of thing really needed guts. *Bluebird* at speed was quite obviously poised on no more than a knife-edge.

As I stood in the boathouse after the run, watching Clive using a wash-leather on her paintwork, I visualised *Bluebird* with her sponsons removed and replaced with wings. She was, in fact, very close to being an aircraft, and I realised that the margin between her being water-borne or air-borne was very finely drawn. I turned to Paul, who was standing nearby.

"I wouldn't do it, would you?" I asked.

He took a long look at the boat as she stood there, water dripping from her hull.

"No," he said, "I'm damned if I would. Come on – let's go and have a drink."

Going for a drink meant driving up to the Sun and standing

with backs to the log fire in the little bar, listening to the chatter about the day's events. And, since this had been a good day, the chatter was plentiful and cheerful. The cameramen were discussing their day's work, David Benson and Norman Luck were in a huddle in the corner, no doubt planning their copy to be sent off to the *Express*. And Bill Jordan was busy with his customary glass of Worthington. When Ken, the bar-man, came in carrying a tray laden with hot 'pasties' there was a sudden surge to the bar, and a call of "Grub's up".

The following day, Sunday, the BBC and the press having broken the news of *Bluebird's* runs the previous day, the crowds came to Coniston in the hope of seeing more runs. However, although Donald and the team had paid a dawn visit to the lake to have a look at the possibilities, the surface remained unsuitable all day, and *Bluebird* did not leave the boathouse.

Donald used the notice-board in the hall at the Sun on which to chalk messages for his team, the most commonly seen being:

"Bluebird team – full stand-by 7.15 am."

This meant a journey down to the lake in the early dawn to study conditions and the team would always be accompanied by a posse of pressmen. All too often, nothing would materialise from the trip, the lake would prove to be choppy or the wind would be too strong. The party would then return for breakfast-, hoping that as the day progressed conditions would improve; that the lake would 'settle'.

It became a habit to look down the length of the lake and to say to each other, with hope and optimism:

"It's settling, I think – don't you?"

The word eventually became used every day and, even though the lake might be in a turmoil with a strong wind whipping across it, someone would be sure to say:

"It's settling, chaps."

On Monday the 12th, Bill Jordan telephoned me again early in the morning, telling me that Donald hoped to go out. Having telephoned Paul, I joined the timekeepers again, accompanied by my wife.

The lake, perfectly still, reflected the ridge of fells behind Coniston village so accurately that a photograph of it would have looked exactly the same, held upside down. It was a rare morning.

Moving off – a superb slow-speed shot of *Bluebird* on a calm Lakeland day *(Paul Allonby)*

The marker buoys had been placed in position the previous day, huge seven feet square slatted boxes, painted red, and lashed, each to two rowing boats. They were moored one at each end of the kilometre. We were now seeing the stage really set.

Again came the call "He's away!" and, within seconds, *Bluebird* flashed past us. On the return run, we could see the sponsons lifting alternately, very rapidly, and could hear a noise, different to anything we had heard before. This was the sound of the sponsons striking the water – port – starboard – port – starboard – at an extremely fast rate.

Norman Buckley, with his experience, probably knew then what we were to learn later: Donald had commenced his second run a little sooner than the last time and had run into the wash of the first run.

After a successful run *(Paul Allonby)*

The speeds on these runs had been 261 mph on the first, and 239 mph on the second. He had cracked 250 mph, and he was very pleased about it. As he climbed from the cockpit at the jetty, and crawled over the engine cover to take up his position at the stern, he paused, on hands and knees, and turning to the press photographers, he said:

"Now's your chance, boys. Here's one for posterity." Climbing down from *Bluebird's* stern, in the boathouse he announced to us all: "The spirit's very high now, very high."

He stood us all a drink in the bar that day, and he enjoyed his game of darts.

11

The Seagull

WE all knew of Donald's many superstitions and indeed they had many times proved to be a very convenient peg on which to hang a story. We began now to have concrete evidence of these superstitions. We saw his teddy bear 'Mr Whoppit', without which he would never undertake a run in either car or boat. We learned that he detested the colour green; indeed, during the first few days Leo Villa had worn a green felt cap which, at Donald's request, soon disappeared to be replaced by a blue woollen ski-cap. I saw the Blue Bird and Saint Christopher plates screwed to the dash-board in the cockpit. I heard of the little Polynesian doll whose tummy Donald would rub from time to time when playing cards. I heard also that one must never wish Donald 'Good luck', that he considered this to be very unlucky; whenever it had been said to him on other projects, apparently something unpleasant had happened, or difficulties had arisen.

Certainly the man had his fair share of superstitions and also apparently a belief in the supernatural. For had he not once consulted a spiritualist medium in an effort to contact his late father?

Knowing all this, when we came to the Tuesday in December which happened to be the thirteenth of the month, we all felt quite sure there would be no runs that day. Although it had dawned crisp with frost, with clear skies and a quiet lake, we told ourselves that *Bluebird* would remain undisturbed in the boathouse, that Donald would find his presence urgently needed elsewhere.

Several of us, sitting in the caravan that morning sipping coffee, were so sure that this would be a day with no action, that we decided to make up a party to go for a walk up the track leading to the summit of the Old Man. It was a lovely morning and we needed the exercise. "Let's go and have a look at the old copper mines," we said.

As I left the caravan to seek out Gerald Harrison and ask him to join us, the E-type pulled up in the yard, followed closely by Keith Harrison's car. Donald walked quickly and purposefully to the workshop, and I followed him. Calling Leo to the door, he pointed to the lake, saying:

"What do you think, Unc?"

Leo took a good long look at the surface, and stared at the branches of the trees to see if they were moving in a breeze, then turning to me he said:

"Would you like to have a run down to Torver – have a look at the lake and come back to report?"

I said I would be pleased, but that I wanted to know exactly what they were looking for.

"Look," said Donald, pointing to the smooth surface near the boathouse. "That's what we are looking for."

Leo grabbed my arm and pointed to a patch of water which was ruffled with tiny waves.

"If it's like that," he said; "it will do."

Donald grinned, shrugged and sent me on my way. Fortunately for my own peace of mind, by the time I reached Torver the whole length of the lake had flattened to a uniform surface.

They waited until I returned and reported, and then Keith Harrison called out:

"Boat crews, come along – let's get afloat."

We were very surprised. There *was* to be a run after all in spite of it being the thirteenth; as the familiar activities of preparation began, I decided to watch from the timekeeping positions.

As I drove along beneath the trees of Grisedale, I could see the Fairlines slowly making their way down the lake, searching for driftwood, and when I reached the wooden platform, I saw that Raoul the timekeeper was there with his watches and batteries, ready to time the run; and Norman Buckley, well mufflered against the cold, stood waiting beside him. Obviously Donald had been busy on the telephone up at the bungalow before he came to the boathouse.

A few minutes later, the perfectly reflected image of the fells was once again disturbed by the swift passage of *Bluebird* as Donald came past us on his first run. Once again the ripples of her passing spread out to the shoreline and the air was disturbed. Soon, before the ripples could return to the centre of the lake, Donald brought her back, and we watched as he flashed past the marker buoy, and in the distance, braked in a flurry of spray.

There would be more runs, we felt quite sure. The conditions were perfect and *Bluebird* seemed to be on top form. Perhaps this could even be a record attempt? We all looked back up the lake, towards the boathouse. Donald would be refuelling now, we thought, and soon we should hear the engine again.

When after twenty minutes, there was neither sight nor sound of the boat, nor any message over the radio, I asked Norman Buckley if he would like me to go back to ask for news.

"Yes," he said. "That would be helpful."

Donald was standing on the rails of the slipway when I arrived. He was alone and his face looked tense. I explained that Norman Buckley was seeking news. Would there be any more runs?

"That poor bloody seagull," he said. Then, after a pause: "What? I'm sorry, old boy. No – it's all right. I'll raise Norman on the RT."

When he returned from the radio truck, I asked him what his reference to a seagull had meant and he took me into the boathouse. Pointing to the rear port sponson spar, he said:

"That's what I meant, old boy. We hit a seagull on the way back."

There was a dent in the spar, very close to its junction with the main hull, but Donald appeared unconcerned about the damage. His more immediate concern, it seemed, was for the bird. Or was it the other thing? Killing a seagull is supposed to be unlucky – and he had killed one on the thirteenth of the month.

He ordered an inspection of the engine, fearing that bits of the disintegrated gull might have been sucked through the air intakes; and the long laborious job of removing the engine cowling commenced.

Donald had also decided, after these two runs, that the Orpheus engine was not getting sufficient fuel, not giving him all the power of which it was capable. His speeds had been 267 mph on the first run south, and 262 mph on the return run, giving him an average of 264.5 mph. He was still below the speed of his existing record.

He telephoned Bristol-Siddeley from the caravan and two of

their technicians travelled up to Coniston that night. The two men, wearing black duffle coats with the name of their company stencilled on the back, commenced work on the engine the following morning, helped by Leo and Maurice, and they got down to the job of finding the cause of Donald's complaints.

For some reason, when the cause had been established and the remedy applied, it was decided not to release details of the work done on the engine. Vague explanations of the fuel problems were offered. I decided that the best way to find out was to ask one of the Bristol-Siddeley boys.

"I don't know what all the mystery is about," he said. "All we have done is to fit a new fuel pump. The old pump wasn't giving of its best. The new pump will. He'll have no more trouble now."

He produced diagrams and 'exploded' drawings of an Orpheus engine and gave me a long dissertation on the subject of its fuel supply. My non-technical mind boggled somewhat at all I heard, but at least I began to appreciate the enormous potential of these engines.

For the next six days, heavy winds returned to Coniston. It became bitterly cold and the space heater in the boathouse worked overtime. The tops of the Old Man and the Yewdale fells were now covered in a thick carpet of snow and the becks which drained the summits of water became white slashes against the brown bracken.

More time was spent talking in the caravan, in the snack bar and in the Sun hotel. And in the bar of the Sun, sipping at a half of bitter near the log fire, the idea that there might be the makings of a book in this Campbell project came to me. The project was now in its sixth week, and they had been weeks packed with incident. It should make quite a story afterwards, the final chapter to tell of the celebration party which would no doubt be held in the Sun after the record had been won. And perhaps Paul Allonby would support such a book with his photographs. I decided to ask Donald's permission, formally, after he had his record.

For I was no close personal friend. I could not claim to know him. I had met him once, briefly, and I had read much about him. Although I was now very much in his company, and had been for six weeks, I was only seeing what everyone else saw and could only guess at the nature of the man. His real friends, those who had known him for years and had accompanied him on all his projects, these were the people to tell me about him.

But all this could come later. There was plenty of time, and the record still had to be won.

*   *   *   *

The bad weather continued from the 15th to the 19th of December. The wind was cutting; thick scarves and ski-caps became the order of the day. The now well-established routine of each day continued. Leo and Maurice would arrive, followed by Louis and Clive. The boathouse and the boat would be inspected, the support boats bailed out and washed down, and if *Bluebird* was not needing their attention, then the team would work on *Jet-Star* in the workshop, making improvements here and there in case there was time to enter her in the coming Boat Show.

Donald would drive up about mid-morning, the usual cigar in his lips, and each time he arrived the atmosphere of the place would change. The activity would become more brisk and, whatever he did, wherever he went, he would be watched. He greeted visitors, showed them *Bluebird,* signed autographs, and once he devoted a full day to two youngsters who had won a newspaper competition, the first prize being 'A day with Donald Campbell at Coniston'.

If he required help with any job, there was no shortage of volunteers and, no matter how small or trivial the task we performed, he would always, towards the end of the day, walk up and say quietly:

"Thanks for all your help today, old boy."

Once I watched him sitting at the end of the jetty, fishing rod in hand, looking pensively at the float bobbing in the water. He caught nothing, but it seemed that for a short time he had forgotten the project and its problems.

If *Jet-Star* was in the water, tied up to the jetty, he would often turn to anyone who stood near, and say:

"Hop in. Let's have a spin."

Everything he did was noted and the cameras worked overtime. Every type of camera. Cine, 16mm. and 9.5mm. Still cameras, 35mm and even the ordinary 'box' camera. They focused on the man Campbell and captured his every mood and expression.

By this time, mid-December, the tension was noticeably

increasing and this was reflected in Donald's face. The lines at
the side of his mouth looked deeper, he frowned more and
smiled less frequently. I caught him gazing through the windows
of the workshop more often, watching the lake and turning to
Leo, asking him to come and have a look.

Christmas was approaching and he wanted his team to be
home for the holiday. Soon it would be the turn of the year, and
the Boat Show was looming up, where perhaps not only *Jet-Star*
but *Bluebird* herself could be displayed.

The questions thrown at him by the press boys were becoming more pointed and demanding. Whenever he passed a group
of them, at least one would call:

"Soon now, Donald?"

Donald would look at the questioner, shrug slightly, as if to
say, "You tell me."

That he succeeded in sustaining the interest of everyone
there, kept them coming day after day, whatever the weather, the
snag or the delay, spoke volumes for the personality of the man.
Indeed as the days clicked away, the interest seemed to increase,
the pressmen became more numerous, and the beaches became
dotted with more and more cars as the sightseers came to
Coniston.

There was no doubt that the project, though it may have got
off to a tepid start, was now capturing the public's attention. The
papers had printed daily reminders that Campbell was still at
Coniston, and *Bluebird* had performed some pretty fast runs.
Soon, it was felt, the record attempt would be made.

So we came to December 19th, when the wind began to show
promise of abating and even the forecast from the met. office
promised better conditions for the following day. Once again the
chalked message on the notice-board at the Sun called the team
to standby at dawn, and Bill Jordan promised to telephone if
things looked promising.

We all separated that evening feeling that this could be it.
Only six more days to Christmas and the forecast sounded good.
What good timing it would be, and what a Christmas present for
Donald and the team if he could get his record now.

The team assembled at the jetty still in the darkness of very
early dawn, liked what they saw, and returned for a quick breakfast and to wait for the light to improve. When they returned and

The morning after: "One bent roofing spar was well down below *Bluebird's* tail fin and she was jammed in." This rear-view shot shows the offset rudder and, right, the tiny water-brake *(Paul Allonby)*

entered the boathouse, they found that once again the gremlins had returned to Coniston.

Bluebird was trapped on her slipway. During the night the winds must have returned, and the rains must have been heavy; the combination of the two had almost completely wrecked the boathouse. The scaffolding had buckled under the enormous weight of water which had collected on the roof, and the structure had partially collapsed. One bent roofing spar was well down below *Bluebird's* tail fin and she was jammed in.

For a brief moment I saw a look of utter bewilderment on Donald's face as he stared at the damage, as though he was thinking:

"What the Devil can happen to me next?"

There had been the business of *Bluebird* getting bogged down at the start, then the ruined engine, the much modified air-intake guards, and the fitting of the lead in her hull. And there had been the wretched weather, which had now done this to him. *Bluebird,* with a still lake waiting for her, with conditions just about perfect, could not be moved.

If Donald Campbell had said there and then "Oh – to hell with it!" and had packed up and returned home, none of us that morning would have been the least bit surprised, nor would we have criticised him.

But Donald had no intention of calling off the project, and perhaps that morning we all realised that he meant to stay at Coniston, no matter how long it took, no matter what the cost to temper and pocket until he had his record.

I held up the sagging roof-sheeting with a boat-hook as he winched *Bluebird* further up the slipway, away from the damaged spar and his grin returned.

"Well, come along," he called. "Let's get the damn thing fixed."

And they did get it fixed. Louis and Clive, clambering about the scaffolding like two chimpanzees, removed bent spars, fitted new lengths, and added stiffening sections to make the structure more rigid. They screwed and unscrewed clamps by the dozen; hands were bruised and the language was colourful – but the job was done.

If the winter picnic parties in their cars on the beaches, and the many people standing around the lake, wondered that day why, when the lake was as calm as a millpond, *Bluebird* was not giving them a display, then Donald Campbell had no means of explaining to them what had happened.

12

Rockets

THERE were four days to go before Christmas; hopes of the record being achieved before the holiday began to recede. The weather, which had shown promise of behaving itself, changed again and gave us an urgent reminder that this was wintertime. The biting easterly winds returned, the clouds lowered over the fell tops and the snowline on the Old Man crept down and down. Films of thin, brittle ice formed on the beaches where the waves nibbled at the shore, and the fields through which the rough track wound its way to the boathouse became hard with frost. It became possible once more to park one's car on the grass without fear of becoming bogged down.

For the cars continued to come each morning and the now well-established routine of the day went on. The camera crews of the various television companies came down, the BBC in a convoy of Ford saloons; Gerald Harrison in his blue '1800'; Tyne Tees in their Land Rover; and Rediffusion in their massive van. The crews would stand around talking, checking and double-checking their equipment and perhaps setting up a tripod and taking shots of this and that, getting background and 'padding' for the films they were making.

The reporters who had been at Coniston since 'Day One' came down in the morning, sniffed the air, looked at the lake, considered the possibilities of the day – and then returned either to their hotel or to the warmth of the snack bar, until more positive action was promised.

We would sit around in the caravan in the morning, sipping coffee, the quality of which by now had become appalling. There was no sugar, there was no milk and the evaporated milk had begun to taste a bit 'off'. We had scrounged so much fresh milk from the patient Arthur Wilson that none of us now had the nerve to ask for more. Only Jim Sherdley seemed to have the knack of creating a reasonable brew from the materials available. My own attempts had been greeted with grimaces so often that I stopped trying. I knew there would be compensation later when the coffee came down from the hotel.

The caravan had begun to look very tatty. The tables were littered with magazines, Donald's large-scale map of Coniston Water with *Bluebird's* course plotted on it lay on one of the seats, and the floor was covered with weeks-old newspaper, muddy and torn. Still, for an hour or two each day until Donald arrived, it provided a shelter and a place in which to gossip.

"No chance now of getting the thing over by Christmas?"

"I doubt it. The forecast is rotten."

"Is Donald going home for the holiday?"

"No idea, but the team is certainly going. Donald has insisted on that."

"Wonder what all this lot's costing him?"

And the estimates, the guesses and the rumours would be tossed around. None of us knew, but it was something to talk about.

When Donald appeared again the atmosphere would change, the tempo would increase, and every move he made was still carefully watched. He was the centre of the whole project, and everyone realised and acknowledged the fact. He continued to answer the questions thrown at him from all sides, but his replies were more perfunctory, his speech more clipped.

He must have been a bit dispirited by now and anxious to have the whole business over and done with. Certainly he never said as much, but one could sense it by the way he talked and the way he darted about the base.

For Paul and I, the project presented few problems. We lived in the district, only some twenty minutes drive away from Coniston, and if necessary we could go home for lunch. Bill Jordan, too, although he had to drive over the mountain passes each day from his home in Millom, was a 'local', as was Jim Sherdley who came in from nearby Ulverston. But for the cameramen and pressmen, who hailed from London, Manchester or Newcastle, it was becoming an anxious time. They had their families to consider, Christmas was imminent and they would like to be at home for the holiday.

What then was in Campbell's mind? Would he, if the weather

proved suitable, actually go for the record on Christmas Day? Some thought yes, others no, but nobody knew. Why, then, didn't the man come right out with it and tell them?

In the end his mind was made up for him; on December 21st, the Swiss timekeepers announced that they were returning to their own country for the Christmas holiday. They had been away from their homes for almost two months and I suspect they were more than a little fed-up. Indeed, one of them was unwell; when one of their expensive watches gave trouble, he, as their team's 'engineer', had to repair it as he lay in bed at the hotel.

I was not present, but I heard that there had been quite a row between Donald and the timekeepers. He wanted them to remain in Coniston over the holiday, and they were quite determined to leave, to go down to London and to fly home.

Donald, having lost the argument, realised that he would now be keeping a lot of people hanging around and he finally announced, at the Sun, that there would be no further tests until December 28th.

There was a sudden exodus from Coniston. The team went home, and the pressmen and the cameramen. The hotel rooms emptied and the trade at the snack bar fell away. The people of Coniston found themselves with a village of their own again and quietly prepared for Christmas.

The project was now fifty-two days old and Donald had still not persuaded *Bluebird* to travel faster than the existing record. The fastest speed achieved had been 264.6 mph and the target was 300 mph.

I began to look back at the history of these record attempts, to study the books written about them. Not only Donald's records, but those of his father, of John Cobb and of Segrave. I found that although some of them had been achieved in a matter of days, most of them had been a lengthy business. The length of this Coniston project was nothing extraordinary. Only the Americans had the knack of announcing an attempt one day, and going out and getting the record the next, or so it seemed.

So the current Coniston project could go on and on, well into 1967 if Donald found it necessary.

On Christmas Eve I drove my wife and daughter into Windermere for a session of shopping, and as I sat waiting for them, Donald, bareheaded in a flurry of falling snow and wearing his blue car-coat, hurried by on the other side of the road. I leaned out of the car window.

"Merry Christmas, Donald," I called.

He turned and, recognising me, came back to the car. As we shook hands, he said:

"Look, old boy, what are you doing? Come into this shop with me will you? I hate this shopping lark. Come and give me moral support."

We entered a chemist's shop, where the customers and the girls behind the counter immediately recognised him, and he made a few small purchases. He was going on to Ulverston he said, one or two people from there had been kind to him and he wanted to say 'thank you'. I have no doubt he was also buying presents for his friends at the Sun.

As we stood chatting outside he told me that the lake had been 'bloody marvellous' that morning and that it would have been 'just right for a run'. We touched briefly on the first time I had met him, so many years ago at Earls Court, and I told him that I had never thought then that one day I would be considering writing a book about him.

"Writing a book – about me? Well, make it pro-Campbell, old boy, and you have my blessing."

Remembering how the boathouse had almost collapsed, I gave him my telephone number in case there should be any emergency during the holiday. I certainly never thought he would be doing any runs at Christmas.

Driving down the main street we passed him again and he spotted my daughter sitting in the back of the car with her three dogs. Above the heads of the passing shoppers, making them all smile, he called:

"What beautiful doggies."

On the evening of Christmas Day, Paul telephoned.

"Did you know the blighter had been out today?" he asked.

"Out where?"

"Out on the Lake, in *Bluebird*."

"How on earth did he manage that? The team's gone home."

"Search me, but he's certainly been out." And indeed he had. With the help of Dr Darbishire and a few friends from the village, Donald had launched *Bluebird* and, on a perfect surface, had taken two unscheduled runs at speeds of over 250 mph.

After many wasted days during which the lake had been unsuitable; after the team and the 'regulars' had left for home; on Christmas day when no one had expected it, *Bluebird* had again been out, and very few had seen her.

I telephoned the Sun on Boxing Day to ask if there was to be a repetition. But nobody thought so, they felt that the previous day's run had been a 'rush of blood to the head' and that tests would begin again on the 28th as Donald had promised.

However, although there was in fact no run on Boxing Day, there certainly was on the following day. Once again, with the help of a handful of friends, he went out again and this time, unofficially and unheralded, he achieved the fastest ever speed at that date – over 280 mph. Untimed and without the official observers being present, he actually broke his own record. Had this been a 'normal' day, with the timekeepers and observers at their stations, the project could well have ended at that point.

During one of the runs this day, *Bluebird* hit a duck, with disastrous results to the bird. The boat was also damaged and when I looked at the damage the next morning, it worried me, and continued to worry me throughout the rest of the project.

Bluebird's two sponsons were 'outrigged' from the main hull, and each was supported by two spars. One high at the front and the other lower down at the rear. When the boat struck the seagull on the 13th, the lower rear port spar was dented very close to its junction with the hull. It did not look to be very serious damage. This time, when *Bluebird* hit the duck, it struck the higher front spar and the damage was very much more obvious, the dent was much larger and adjacent to a joint in the spar's metal sheathing.

Although I was trained as an engineer, I claim no knowledge of aerodynamics or hydrodynamics, subjects of which *Bluebird's* design had been the very essence. However, looking at the damage, I visualised the air being disturbed when meeting this dent, and instead of flowing smoothly over the top and bottom of the spar, being 'broken up' as it met a configuration which was no longer smooth.

This so niggled at my mind that I asked Maurice if he did not consider it would alter the air-flow. He said he would have thought so, but that the Skipper had decided to leave it alone.

Paul was also very interested and took a photograph of the damage.

Ken Norris had travelled up to Coniston from the south and we were all very interested to see the man who had been so instrumental in the design and building of the boat. Slim and boyish, with a pencil thin black moustache, he looked very little older than he did on photographs I had seen of him taken on earlier projects. He bustled around, leather document case in hand, and spent one day standing in *Bluebird's* cockpit, wielding a tube of Bostik, trying to stop water entering.

Looking at Norris I recalled that it was he who finally solved the problem of the vibrations Donald had felt in the *Bluebird* car in Australia in 1964; ignoring the comments and snide remarks about Campbell's courage, he had proved that Donald was right. He had discovered that the wet salt, thrown up from the track during a number of runs, had crystallised in uneven lumps on the wheel rims, throwing them out of balance. On the next morning, fresh, salt-free wheels having been fitted, Donald went out and drove the car faster than anyone had driven before.

It was also Ken Norris who, with Leo Villa, had been first at the scene of Donald's crash with the car at Bonneville Salt Flats and had seen him so seriously injured. He had stood, looking at the wreckage, believing that Donald had reached the end of his record-breaking career. But here he was at Coniston helping him with yet another project in a career which had continued after all.

After Norris left the base to return home, we began to talk about the birds we were now seeing in increasing numbers, flying low over the lake and floating on its surface. Already there had been two 'collisions', with the gull and the duck; obviously these birds were going to be something of a hazard. I suggested that shot-guns be fired in the air just before each run to scare the birds away. Donald agreed and it was tried, a villager bringing a selection of guns to the boathouse. It was found, however, that although the birds flew up into the air when a gun was fired, the explosion was insufficiently loud to give them a real scare and they soon settled back on the surface.

Donald then sent Louis off in the brake to Huddersfield, where he visited the works of the Standard Fireworks Company. When he returned he brought with him some very lethal-looking high-powered rockets and these proved to be the answer to the problem.

The following morning Donald drove a stake, into which staples had been hammered, into the earth outside the workshop. He placed a rocket in the staples and lit the touch-paper. The rocket fizzed, roared and shot up high over the lake. There was a staccato crack of a dozen explosions, and birds flew up from all angles, seagulls, ducks, the local chaffinches, the lot. And they did not return for a long time.

Keith Harrison, who had appointed himself chief pyrotechnician suggested that when *Bluebird* was ready for a run, I fire a rocket from the northern timekeeper's position, and that someone else fire one from the south end. In fact, this was never put into practice and the rockets were fired from the support launches.

Thus the days of waiting, after Christmas, were fully occupied with something or other, and the talk and the gossip continued.

"Nice if he got the thing on New Year's Day, wouldn't it?"

"Nicer still if he got it today. I'm going to bed for two months when this show's over."

"Wonder what these press boys will do after all this?"

"Back to Vietnam and Harold Wilson, I suppose."

"And the TV boys, what about them?"

"Soccer matches, horse racing and riots in Trafalgar Square."

13

Traffic Jams

PAUL and I sat in the car at the viewpoint, looking down the full length of Coniston Water. We could see the huge marker buoys at their stations marking the start and finish of the measured kilometre. They were rolling gently as their rowing-boat 'pontoons' rose and fell to the movement of the water. Looking at the lake from here, there seemed to be very little distance, very little room beyond the far marker buoy in which to stop a boat from a speed of 300 mph. And that sharp bend at the far end, where Peel Island could be seen at the left, that must be the trickiest bit of the lot. Donald had explained that he had in fact a mile of water beyond the island in which to brake, but from where we sat it looked as though the lake tapered off into a river at that point. What had Donald said?

"Coniston is about five miles long and half a mile wide. When we pass the last buoy, having completed the kilometre, we have about two miles of water left. Peel Island looms up on our left, and there are some rocks on the right. We are doing about 200 miles per hour when we go through this gap. Then we enter a bay, perhaps a mile long, in which we stop, turn around, and prepare to return. If we are refuelling, then we meet the dory down there. If not, we either wait, until the wake of the first run has completely subsided, and the lake settled again, or we come back fairly soon before the wake rolls back on to the course."

Well – we had heard him describe it and indeed we had seen him do it. It still looked a pretty tricky business to us.

We pressed on to the boathouse. There was perhaps a chance we might see him do it again today. The lake might settle in the afternoon.

But eight more days were to pass before we saw *Bluebird* on the lake again.

The press boys came back to Coniston, and the cameramen,

and this time there were new faces to be seen at the boathouse. The reporters from the 'heavies' and 'glossies' and American magazines, sensing that the big story would not be long delayed, came to get in on the act and joined those who had been with the project from the start. The crowd which gathered each morning was much larger, and it became difficult to find space in which to park a car. More and more people who had really no right to be there found their way down the track or across the fields. Women with cameras followed Donald around everywhere he went, snapping him in every pose, pestering him to sign their autograph books or any bit of paper they happened to have with them.

Donald kept his patience, but some of the press boys did not. One morning when there was a seething mass of people milling around all over the place, and the yard was jammed with cars, one of the reporters grabbed Bill Jordan's arm.

"Look, I thought you were supposed to keep this place in order. What the hell are all these women doing here. Get them out, we chaps have a job to do."

So Bill and Jim got busy, asking to see press cards, notes of authority or other identification which would show a person had a right to be there. If none was forthcoming, then the person was shepherded out of the yard and asked not to return; they were told to go round to the beach on the other side of Church Beck, where they could watch without getting in the way. But it was no use – they all came back the following day.

The interest was quickening. The news of the fast Christmas run had been printed and broadcast, and all those who could wished to be present when the record attempt was made.

On Thursday December 29th Donald told a press gathering at the Sun that if he gained his record before midnight on New Year's Eve, then he would receive sufficient money from two American companies to cover forty per cent of the total cost of the project. So the rumour which we had heard some time ago was confirmed.

And the talk and the gossip started up again.

"Nine o'clock Saturday morning, that's my bet. Just in time to win the money, and just in time for the Honours List."

"No, I don't see Donald getting his knighthood – those days have gone."

"Bit of a devil, taking money from the Americans when he's supposed to be doing it for Britain."

"Well, they have it to spare and there's no one here rushing to help is there?"

There was indeed a stand-by on the morning of New Year's Eve.

Donald and the team assembled at the boathouse, Bill gave me his early morning call, but when we all arrived at the base we could see, in the half light, that there was a 'popple' on the lake and a cold wind was blowing over the surface. Once again Donald's party returned for breakfast at the Sun and the snack bar opened its doors to the bacon and egg brigade. Once again we lit the gas fire in the caravan, read the papers and pretended to enjoy the coffee. The lake might settle later, but there would be no run that morning.

This was the anniversary of Donald's existing record, gained in *Bluebird* on Lake Dumbleyung in Western Australia in 1964; it did not pass unnoticed. Donald stood drinks all round in the bar of the Sun at lunch-time and he was in very good form. Lady Aitken had returned to Coniston for the New Year's holiday and a darts match was arranged: *Bluebird* team versus the *Express*. Donald and Louis played against Lady Aitken and David Benson, and the *Bluebird* team won, Donald getting a 'double one' to finish.

There was an air of greater excitement that day, a sense of the imminence of the record attempt. The opening, on the Wednesday, of the 1967 Boat Show was discussed and the question of the possibility of Donald getting *Bluebird* down there in time to put her on display was raised.

We all still hoped that it would be possible for *Bluebird* to go out that day, and we kept glancing out of the window to see if the wind had died down, and asked everyone who entered the bar if there was any sign of the lake settling. For Donald to beat his record on the same day he had gained his existing one, exactly two years ago, and be able to collect the American 'award', would have been a fitting climax to the long weeks of waiting.

But it was not to be. For the rest of the day the lake remained unsuitable and the wind continued to blow down off the Old Man. If Donald was disappointed, he showed no sign of it. But we were disappointed for him.

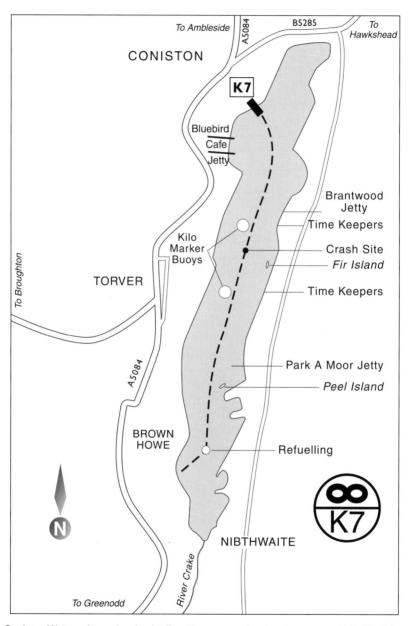

Coniston Water, after a drawing by Ray Hewartson, showing the course of K7. The lake is 5¼ miles long, half a mile wide and 180ft (54.5 metres) deep

A new notice appeared on the board in the hall that day. Chalked by Donald, it read:

> *To all Shutter-bugs and Scribes, and their birds.*
> *There will be a fancy-dress party at the Sun tonight.*
> *Hostess: Lady Aitken.*
> *Host: Old Misery.*

And a party there was, going on into the small hours. Donald, dressed as a French Chef, with black paper moustache stuck to his lip, toasted the 'gentlemen of the press' at midnight.

"I know," he said, "that you are all waiting for me to break my neck."

The next morning saw no rush down to the lake, no stand-by message written on the notice-board. Breakfast was only toyed with, and recumbent bodies could be seen sprawling in the easy chairs in the lounge. It had been a hectic night, and tongues were furred and heads heavy. I made the mistake of telephoning the Sun quite early that morning and my question as to whether there would be 'anything doing' was greeted with a groan. I should have known better.

But the crowds came to Coniston. It was a public holiday, and the beaches and the roads around the lake became thick with cars. People streamed across the field from the boating beach and soon the bank on the other side of Church Beck was packed with onlookers, peering across at the boathouse from which hung a green tarpaulin, hiding *Bluebird* from their view. When Donald did appear, there was a buzz of excitement and camera shutters began clicking.

I suggested to him that he laid a plank across the beck, and permitted them all to come in and that he charge them half-a-crown.

"It would almost pay for the project, old boy, wouldn't it?" he said. "Look, I've a better idea: you get a guitar, Keith can get on the drums, and I'll sing. We'll keep 'em entertained. Who says Campbell's not popular?"

He took *Jet-Star* out and drove around the lake, sensing that the crowd would like to have a good look at him, and one small boy, standing on the beach with the controls in his hand, sent a radio-controlled model of *Bluebird*, a perfect replica, zooming around the bay, as if to say, 'I can, if you can't.'

There was no run that day. Although the waters did settle in the late afternoon, the light had gone and a mist appeared down the lake towards the south end.

On the following day, the Monday, the two Bristol-Siddeley technicians appeared on the base again; once more the many snap-fasteners of the engine cowling were unscrewed and the cowling was removed from the boat. We learned later in the day that Donald, after his 280 mph runs on the Tuesday after Christmas, had felt that *Bluebird* had been flat out at that speed, that the Orpheus had been giving him all its available power in its present state of tune. And Donald, chasing 300, wanted the power increased, wanted the engine 'tweaking' to give him the extra boost. The two experts worked on the engine and gave it the extra sting for which he asked.

Donald then announced that he was going to run another static test, but he was very anxious and worried about the numbers of people around the place.

"Please ask them to move well away from the boathouse," he said. "Tell them to stand on the jetty and keep absolutely clear of the jet-stream. I am going to run it right up to the top."

Bluebird was again shackled fore and aft, loose items of equipment were removed from the path of the air suction, and the more knowledgeable of the onlookers began to stuff pieces of cotton wool in their ears. The television cameramen took up positions which would enable them to film the jet-stream, and Paul Davies of CBC, more daring than the rest, mounted his tripod down at the end of the jetty right in the line of fire. He did not realise this; nor did we – until Donald started up the engine and slowly began to apply more and more power. The engine began to scream at full revolutions and the water behind the boat was deeply furrowed with the force of the jet. Spray was thrown right across to the other side of the lake and the air shimmered.

We turned, to see Paul, bent double, clinging with one hand to a post on the jetty and hanging on with the other to his camera and tripod, which had collapsed. Polythene sheeting with which he had shielded the camera lens from the spray now covered his face and we were anxious about his breathing. There he crouched, full in the path of the jet-stream, clinging on like grim death. His woollen cap flew off into the lake, and any minute now, we thought Paul would follow it. Just when he must have been at his very last gasp, when his fingers were about to slip from the post, Donald throttled the engine down. We reached Paul to find him grinning as if he had fully enjoyed himself. Despite his precarious position, he must somehow have kept his camera turning, for he said he was all right and had got his picture.

Donald was very concerned to hear about this incident and he immediately went out in *Jet-Star* to recover Paul's cap, which was bobbing on the surface a hundred yards away.

In the late afternoon, the surface of the lake became glass-like and hurried preparations were made for a run, before the light faded. When this became obvious to the crowds, there was excitement and a rush for vantage points. *Bluebird* was fuelled, and Donald waited for a radio message to tell him that conditions at the south end were right, that the timekeepers and observers were in position. But the minutes passed, and the minutes became half an hour, and there was no news. What the devil was wrong? Finally, when the daylight had faded, Norman Buckley and Andrew Brown drove back into the yard.

Because of the traffic on the eastern road around the lake, the two observers had been unable to reach the timekeeping positions: could the police do something about it?

Bill Jordan and Jim Sherdley set off in the police Land Rover to see what could be done; one hour later, in the dusk of the evening, they returned looking very harassed.

They told us that the road – running the full length of Coniston Water from High Nibthwaite at the south end to Tent Lodge at the north – had been jammed with cars, two deep in many places on the narrow, winding road, and that the only way to sort out the mess was to wait until dark, until there was no further possibility of *Bluebird* being seen. The cars would then leave for home.

The police were very concerned about the possibility of a repetition the following day. Many people would be taking the Tuesday off work as part of the New Year's holiday and the same thing could happen again. Superintendent Abbott thought that it would be unfair to seal off the road to traffic and decided that it should be constantly patrolled to keep the traffic moving or parked well off the road.

I drove along the road the following morning and found that, this time, the cars were parked in an orderly manner, on the beaches, in the lay-bys and up the tracks into Grisedale Forest, and the road was being kept clear by a constable on a motorcycle. This was at nine o'clock in the morning. The crowds were already here. This was the atmosphere at Coniston on Tuesday January 3rd. The record run was imminent.

Again, for the third day running, the lake, having been ruffled all day, calmed and flattened, and began to reflect its surroundings, in the late afternoon. This time, however, it was half an hour too late. Although Donald peered down the length of the course from the beach, there was insufficient visibility at the far end, nothing on which he could sight his run. He had told me he sighted on a small square, green field away down at Brown Howe at the south end, and I could certainly see no such target. Nor could he; he turned, looking apologetically at the crowds on the shoreline, shrugged his shoulders, got into the E-type, and drove away.

We were all agreed now that this must be the week for the record attempt. The weather conditions were much more favourable and we heard that the met. office had given Donald cheering news. The last few days had been crisp and sharp, with blue skies. It was just the wind, which continued to blow a little too long each day. When that stopped, when the air became still, *Bluebird* would be out.

Paul and I and many of the other 'old hands' had earlier decided that, when the run was made, we would stay up at the boathouse. We had already seen runs from the timekeeping positions and did not feel like becoming involved in the mad rush back to the boathouse when it became known that the record was won. We wanted to be at the jetty, when *Bluebird* came back, and we wanted to see Donald's face as he stepped from the cockpit; we wanted to shake his hand, to pat him on the back, before he became surrounded by admirers and submitted to interview.

We also planned to be at his celebration party up at the Sun afterwards.

14

End of Project

DONALD'S bid to persuade *Bluebird* to skim across the
surface of Coniston Water at 300 mph and thus, perhaps,
push the world record out of the reach of the Americans, was
now sixty-four days old. His project had seen the passing of an
old year and greeted the coming of a new. And what days they
had been.

The previous evening, January 3rd, Paul and I had been drink-
ing with Donald at the Sun doing a bit of re-capping: looking
back over the days we had spent at Coniston and calculating the
probable number of times we had driven past the Drunken Duck
on our way to Coniston and back. Paul suggested a hundred and
thirty, but I said I had been home for lunch on a few occasions,
and that it was probably nearer a hundred and forty. Eighteen
miles, there and back – nine times one hundred and forty – hmm
– one thousand two hundred and sixty miles, through November, December and into January. It was more mileage than I
would usually do during the winter.

And what had we seen? *Bluebird's* first engine written off; a
new one installed; all that messing about with the air intake
guards; the fitting of the lead to balance her weight; and, above
all, the weather. We had certainly seen that. Wind, rain, snow,
hail, frost, ice and mist, and then the same, all over again. And
still Donald Campbell came up for more. Ah well, it shouldn't be
long now. Perhaps tomorrow, eh? Sure enough, when tomorrow
came, Bill telephoned at seven in the morning.

"Coming? I won't see you until it's all over, I'll be down at the
south end, refuelling with Louis."

The drive over was very little different to any of the others. It
was earlier than usual, so it was darker and I nearly ran into a
sheep straying on the fell road. The corners were a bit slippery

Donald in full regalia, before settling into the cockpit *(Paul Allonby)*

and I was reminded that my front tyres were getting smooth. Must do something about those when all this is over, I thought.

It was too dark to see the lake properly when I reached the viewpoint, but the lights were on in the boathouse, and in the army radio truck. I could see them reflected in the water. When I switched off the engine for a few minutes to watch the daylight creeping over the Old Man, I could hear the phut-phut-phut of the compressor away in the distance, a sound that had been constantly in the background during the whole project. As I sat there, a white Mini passed me, going down the hill. Probably Geoff Hallawell, I thought, going down from his cottage at Sawrey in his wife's car. He had told me that a big-end had gone in his TVR: He'll be going out with Keith Harrison in one of the Fairlines.

I was much too early. Driving down, I stopped at the gate guarding the track to the boathouse, but could see no signs of activity down there. They would all be back at the Sun having breakfast I guessed. The usual routine. I drove into the village, bought a couple of newspapers and returned to the caravan to read them.

Yes, it had been Geoff, as I thought. He was sitting in the Mini sorting out his camera gear. And Paul, the signals corporal, was there, swinging away at the starting handle of the army Land Rover, trying to get the thing to start, so he too could go for breakfast.

The same old short paragraphs in the papers. The weather had once again prevented Donald Campbell from making further trials, although the attempt on the record could be 'any time now'.

There was not even any instant coffee left in the jar on the sink now, so I left the caravan to stroll along the jetty. I was surprised to find so many people down there. Keith Harrison was already on board one of the Fairlines, loading rockets and other gear, and there was much fiddling about with cameras amongst the group standing around. One of the boys from a press agency strolled up and pointed towards the grass at the side of Arthur Wilson's house; there were two swans there. They waddled towards the water, launched themselves into it and paddled towards the side of the jetty.

"We haven't seen those before – aren't they supposed to be unlucky?"

"I wouldn't know. At least they're not albatrosses."

The light was now quite good and we could see a fair distance down the lake. It looked flat and oily. With the coming of daylight, the group, fairly subdued up to then, began to talk amongst themselves.

"This is no false alarm is it? This looks like the day."

"Yes, let the lad get it over and done with. Just in time for the Boat Show."

"They'd never get it down in time would they?"

"Of course they would. They'd take it down overnight."

"Are you staying here for the run?"

"No, I think I'll drive round the other side and I think I'll go now, before the crowds come."

Soon, the cars began to return from Coniston, bumping down the track, entering the yard, and being manoeuvred until a parking place could be found. Within minutes the yard was full

Donald gives the "Ready to go" signal *(Paul Allonby)*

and the later arrivals began to park on the fields outside. Leo and Maurice in the Vauxhall arrived, followed by Louis and Clive in the brake, and these two began to roll up the green tarpaulin which hung down at the slipway end of the boathouse. We knew then that *Bluebird* was indeed going out.

I did not hear the call 'Skipper's here' this morning. Suddenly he arrived. The blue E-type pulled up in the yard and Donald, in the familiar car-coat and overalls, stepped out. The usual grins, nods and winks, the usual darting walk. The start of a usual sort of day, except that this time he was taking the boat out.

Preparations for the launching began. The tail-pipe cover was unclipped and removed, the engine of the Land Rover which drove the winch was started, the length of steel pipe which prevented the rear wheels of the launching cradle from moving was withdrawn. Clive clipped a thin rope line to the stern of the boat and stood on the jetty holding the other end,

Donald, standing in the cockpit, gave a signal, the winch started turning and *Bluebird*, with slight, hesitant jerks, began moving towards the water. When she floated free, Maurice with a boat-hook and Clive holding the line, gently eased her round the end of the jetty until she pointed at a forty-five degree angle towards the centre of the lake.

I watched as Donald put on his tiny life jacket, the oxygen mask, his leather helmet which held the radio earphones; then I walked around the boathouse to the beach which afforded the view of the course. As I watched him from there, Donald reached for his jet pilot's helmet, which had been presented to him by Neville Duke, and settling it on his head, he sat waiting for the radio message from the south end, telling him that all was ready. Within seconds, Maurice had unhooked the boat-hook and the line was unclipped. Donald drew the cockpit cover towards him and slammed it shut over his head, and we heard the hiss and whine of the engine being started.

Slowly *Bluebird* moved away from the jetty, and Donald taxied her towards the deeper water, passing quite close to the beach on which we stood. He lined her up, sighting her down the lake, and began to apply power. Clouds of spray were thrown up, *Bluebird* lifted to her sponsons and Donald reached what he had called 'the critical stage'.

What had he said?

"This needs a delicate manoeuvre. We are doing seventy. Apply brake sharply, turn left just as sharply, and up comes the back of the boat."

Bluebird came up to her planing points like a ballet dancer and streaked away into the distance, engine screaming and the familiar comet-tail of spray stretched out behind her.

Looking at her through binoculars I noticed the optical illusion which Donald had described at some time. *Bluebird* appeared to be off course, to be crabbing away to the left. But she wasn't, she was dead on course and travelling as straight as an arrow. I watched her flash down the measured kilometre and, far in the distance beyond Peel Island, I saw the spray fly up as Donald applied the water brake.

"'That didn't seem terribly fast did it?" asked Jim Sherdley. "But of course you can't tell from this angle."

Soon, perhaps only four minutes later, she was on her way back, and this time she appeared to be on a different course, much closer to the eastern shoreline. Unobscured now by the jet-stream, I could see clearly the blue shape, hurtling towards us like a projectile.

From my viewpoint, it seemed to me that she had passed the last marker buoy when she left the water and took to the air – as if entering her natural element, as if this was the purpose for which she was built – inexorably it seemed. She climbed into the air, for perhaps fifty feet, hovered momentarily, and then plummeted down to the surface of the lake in a vast eruption of water. For fractions of a second – long enough for me to breathe "Thank God he's all right" – she floated on the surface. Then she was gone.

There were moments of complete, numbed silence. Then, close to me a woman whimpered. Someone said:

"He'll be okay. He has half an hour's oxygen."

I ran to the radio truck, where a small knot of people had gathered. The static crackled – then came the message:

"There's been a complete accident. No details. Over."

We had all known this could happen. Donald himself always knew it was on the cards each time he took *Bluebird* out. Now that it had happened, no one believed it. We walked around with baffled expressions, seeking perhaps, from someone, reassurance. The talk of the half-hour oxygen supply went the rounds.

Minutes later, it seemed, complete realisation dawned on the pressmen and there was a crazy scramble for the two telephones in the caravan. They became then the 'hottest' lines in the country, so hot that the telephone exchange could not deal with the demand. I stood with Gerald Harrison as he scribbled on his 'story-board', waiting for a telephone to be vacated. Norman Buckley and Andrew Brown drove into the yard and stepped from the car, pale-faced and drawn.

"Is there any hope, Andrew?"

"Not a chance, I'm afraid. I fear he must be dead. There is no trace."

I grabbed a telephone as it became free and held it for Gerald. As he read out his story to the BBC I heard for the first time what

Top: heading for disaster – sponsons high out of the water, *Bluebird* is estimated to be
skimming across Coniston Water at 300 mph, but decelerating *(Geoffrey Hallawell)*
Bottom: *Bluebird* then takes to the air *(News International)*

Top: *Bluebird* turns almost a complete somersault before one of her sponsons strikes
the surface of the lake. **Bottom:** *Bluebird* strikes the lake at 8.58am and then cartwheels
along the surface before breaking up *(both photographs – News International)*

the speeds of the runs had been; 297 mph on the first run, and well over 300 mph just before the crash.

Replacing the receiver, Gerald glanced at his watch.

"Where's your car, Arthur?" he asked.

We switched the car radio on and stood listening as, seconds later, the news he had just recorded was repeated back to us. It was just ten-thirty.

Those to whom news was their stock-in-trade began to do their job. The television teams started interviewing people. Andrew Brown and Dr Darbishire were interviewed, Harry Griffin and I, and then Arthur Wilson, who said he was convinced that something flew off *Bluebird* as she crashed. All had their theories, but I had none. I did worry away to myself about that wretched dent in the spar. Did that have anything to do with it?

Jim Sherdley walked up.

"They've sent for divers," he said. "They're on their way from Barrow now."

It occurred to me that there had been no provision made for such a disaster. Had Donald been thrown clear into the water, those in the support boats could have plucked him out. But if he had gone down with the boat, there was nothing they could do. They were helpless.

We could see the boats, cruising around over the scene of the crash, searching, searching. A message came that they had found Donald's helmet, his life-jacket and Mr Whoppit, the teddy-bear, floating on the surface. And an hour later one of the boats came in to the jetty towing a half section of one of *Bluebird's* sponsons. Soon the other half was brought in, and a battered piece of metal on which was painted *Bluebird's* registration number. Then came Donald's seat and with it came the realisation that he must have been thrown out of the cockpit.

Perhaps it was the sight of that seat as it lay propped up against a post on the jetty which brought home to us the full horror of the crash. And the full knowledge that we should not be seeing Donald again.

The coffee came down from the hotel as usual; as we stood sipping it in the workshop, I asked Gerald:

"What were Donald's last words, exactly?"

He passed me his story-board, pointing to his notes.

"That's just as it came over the radio," he said. And I looked at the words which, though very brief, told the whole story:

"She's tramping ...

"Full power on ...

"I'm going."

Paul Davies and a BBC cameraman cruised to the jetty in their launch and threw more evidence of the crash on to the wet planking; then they set off again for the scene.

Leo Villa, pale and haggard, accompanied by Connie Robinson's son 'Robby' came next in one of the Fairlines. Immediately Leo was lost to sight in a crowd of pressmen.

I sat later in the caravan answering the telephone which rang incessantly. Norman Buckley and Andrew Brown entered, saying that they were going to telephone Tonia. As these were Donald's friends and their task a very private matter, I left the caravan. However, a television crew crowded into the doorway, saying,

"Come along; they're going to phone Tonia."

There was to be no privacy. Everything that day was news.

We all stood around, watching, talking and the consoling thought in all our minds was that Donald would have known very little about it. That it would all have been over in a fraction of a second.

There was a very large gathering in the Sun at lunchtime that morning. We crowded into the lounge to watch the film of the crash on television. Those of us who had remained at the boathouse, and had seen it happen, head-on, at a distance, were now able to see how very dramatic it had been: how *Bluebird* had sped in the north-south direction, at a speed of 297 mph, and had then returned, at 300 mph plus, until, some 140 feet from the last kilometre marker, she had soared gracefully into the air and, in a perfect arc, had somersaulted back to the water, to roll and roll, rapidly, perhaps half a dozen times. We saw her settle on the surface, briefly, and then vanish from sight.

As we returned to the bar, Paul, the signals corporal, said:

"My God. I never knew it was like that."

A genial, burly BBC cameraman, who some weeks earlier had accused me of 'taking the mickey' when describing in a cine magazine article the making of a television film at Coniston, walked up to me, and said quietly:

"'Now you see how the professionals do it, old son."

It was indeed a remarkable film and perhaps that taken by the independent television team, which we saw later in the day, was even better. They had filmed from a slightly different angle and the result was even more spectacular.

In the bar, I was given confirmation of a story, snatches of which I had heard in the morning at the boathouse. David Benson and Keith Harrison told how, the previous evening, Donald had played a form of Russian patience; he had turned up the Ace of Spades and followed it with the Queen of Spades. Donald had said:

"You know, Mary, Queen of Scots turned these same two up just before she was beheaded. Someone is going to get the chop – and I pray to God it isn't me. But if it is, I hope I'm going ruddy fast at the time."

I heard how, as he sat in *Bluebird's* cockpit before the start of the first run, he had said:

"I'm still worried about those cards, you know."

There was a press conference in the hotel that afternoon and Norman Buckley was bombarded with questions. Most of these came from pressmen who had only just arrived, having heard the news in the morning. Those who had been with Donald throughout the project were silent.

"Was the surface of the lake absolutely right for such an attempt?"

"Yes, in my opinion conditions were perfect."

"That business of putting lead castings into the hull: was that a bit of a 'do-it-yourself' affair?"

"No, it was not. These were engineers and they knew what they were doing."

"Was it a do or die attempt?"

"I think not."

It solved nothing, it gave no positive lead as to what had really happened. But it provided copy for the papers.

The search of the disaster area continued late into the afternoon until darkness fell, but only a few small pieces of debris were found, floating amongst the hundreds of polythene air buoyancy packs which had come to the surface. Of Donald's body there was no sign.

As the search boats returned at the end of the day, to be

moored at the jetty for the night, I stood looking at the E-type Jaguar standing in the yard, Donald's blue car-coat flung over the passenger seat. And at *Bluebird's* wheeled cradle, standing deep in the water at the end of the slipway. I turned to find Maurice Parfitt looking too. For a long moment we stared at each other. Then as I had so many times before, I said:

"Cheerio, Maurice."

"Cheerio – see you in the morning."

Habits acquired over a period of nine weeks die hard. The drive home that night, with Paul's car close behind, was much slower. I thought back to the early morning, before *Bluebird* was launched. Had there been any difference about the morning, about Donald? I could remember only one slight difference. When he strode from the workshop to the boathouse, a small group of pressmen made as though to question him. Usually he would have stopped and answered them. This time he put out his arm and brushed right past them. He obviously wished to get on with the job in hand.

15

"A Patriotic Boy"

IF Donald Campbell could have seen the headlines which were
blazoned in the papers the following day, he might well have
chuckled, and no doubt he would have repeated his question of
New Year's Day – "Who says Campbell isn't popular?" For
Donald certainly got his publicity. His had been a spectacular
life and it ended in a spectacular manner. The press, radio and
television people recognised this and let the whole world see
how he had died. And, although we had been there and had seen
it happen, it needed this vast collation of printed word, picture,
film and eye witness account to give us a full understanding of
what had actually happened. For we had been too close to the
thing.

Donald, after breakfasting on cornflakes and coffee laced with
brandy, had launched *Bluebird* at 8.40 am. As we had stood
watching him, he had radioed Leo Villa who was stationed along
the course in one of the Fairlines:

"Leo, how is the water?"

"There's a slight swell, Skipper, but it could have been caused
by our own boat."

Keith Harrison, also down the course, had confirmed that
there was a slight swell. Then Donald gave his instructions.

"Okay all stations. Rockets – fire one."

The rocket on the first boat had soared into the air and, at the
sound of its explosions, the second rocket further down the
kilometre was fired. It was now 8.45 and Donald asked if the
timekeepers were ready. They replied that they were.

"Right," he said. "Here we go", and at 8.47 the jet-engine
roared into life and the first run commenced. Excitedly, over the
radio, his voice was heard:

"Full house – full house."

The first run completed, he taxied *Bluebird* to line her up for the return run and received from Andrew Brown over the radio the message he wanted to hear: "Tango to Skipper – Tango to Skipper – Plus 47 – Plus 47."

This was a simple code. Using 250 as zero, anything above or below this speed was 'plus' or 'minus'. Thus when Donald heard 'Plus 47' he knew that his speed for the first run had been 297 mph. He would know, too, that for him to achieve his stated target of 300 mph he must return at a speed of 303 mph.

Eyewitness accounts vary only slightly about the second run. It commenced at 8.51 and *Bluebird* this time came closer to the eastern shoreline. As she entered the measured kilometre, she was moving very fast, and already her starboard sponson could be seen riding clear of the water. Keith Harrison described it:

"I saw her starboard sponson lift about twelve inches from the water. I could not recall ever seeing that happen before. I shouted to myself 'For Christ's sake – slow down!' and then I saw the nose start to lift very, very slowly, in fact she looked like a whacking great blue bird trying to fly off the water. Then she seemed to stand on her tail ..."

So to Donald, only a few feet from attaining his eighth world water speed record, came disaster.

Reports of the estimated speed of the second run varied considerably. Some said 320 mph, others 350 mph and it was even suggested that *Bluebird* could have been moving at about 400 mph when she crashed. Later analyses suggest that such high speeds were very unlikely.

Then came the speculation as to what had happened to Donald. Did he die during the boat's upward flight? Did the long drawn out sigh, which was the last sound heard from his radio, suggest that the G-forces had expelled the air from his body? Was he flung from the cockpit during the somersault? Or did he die when the boat crashed to the water? Why was it that his helmet, his shoes and his life jacket came, so soon, to the surface? Where was Donald Campbell's body?

Divers from Vickers' shipyards at Barrow-in-Furness arrived on the scene during the late morning, but they found that the depth was too great, working as they were without pressurised suits. On the following day, a team of divers from the Royal Naval Dockyards at Rosyth arrived, led by Lieutenant Commander Futcher.

They assembled their equipment on the jetty. Black rubber
dinghies powered by black outboard engines. Black diving suits
and helmets. Air bottles and pumps. Lengths of rubber piping
and lengths of rope. And rubber buoys, to mark the position of
anything they were to find. A large cylindrical decompression
chamber was installed in the workshop to be ready should one of
the team be afflicted with the hazard all divers fear, the 'bends'.

With the arrival of the divers, the base became a different
place. The workshop, the boathouse and the jetty, which had
been the scene of bustle and activity for so many weeks, which
had seen crowds of pressmen, cameramen and sightseers, and
had enjoyed an atmosphere of fun and expectation, now looked
sombre. There were too many reminders. The slipway stood
empty, the gossiping groups had gone, there were no cameras or
tripods lying around, nor was the blue E-type standing in its
familiar place near the caravan. The door of the caravan swung
idly on its hinges, but there was no one entering or leaving, and
the telephone no longer shrilled. The old damaged engine still
lay on the ground near the workshop, looking shabby and
battered – and in some way, slightly sinister. And there was
another reminder, something I had not noticed before. In the
grass and on the well-trodden earth, were dozens of gold tips and
tiny plastic holders from the many cigars which had been
smoked there over the weeks. Donald himself had set the trend;
from the first day he arrived, cigar in mouth, team members,
pressmen and television crews had started smoking cigars. Now,
as I stood watching the divers prepare for their task, I noticed
that they were all smoking cigarettes. The place had changed.

On the first day of the search, working in freezing conditions
140 feet below the surface, they found a large section of
Bluebird's hull, the section from the back of the cockpit to the
stern, in which the engine was housed. *Bluebird* had broken in
two.

As the search continued, Donald's widow, Tonia, arrived at
the lakeside, dressed in fur coat, black trouser suit and wearing
dark glasses. She had flown from London to Walney and from
there had been given a police escort to Coniston. She stood
gazing for long minutes across the water towards the two rubber
dinghies, where the divers were working. Although obviously

After the crash, left to right: Andrew Brown, Maurice Parfitt and Leo Villa *(Paul Allonby)*

deeply distressed, she thanked the press, the police and all concerned with the search before leaving.

As she was driven away, a lone Royal Air Force Vulcan bomber flew low over the surface of the lake and, when over the scene of the crash, its wings were dipped three times in tribute. Other small private aircraft flew over the lake, circling and circling, one coming so low that its landing wheels skimmed the surface.

Donald's mother, Lady Campbell arrived in Coniston and was taken down to the boathouse, where she stood quietly on the jetty gazing out across the water. Messages of condolence began to stream into the Sun Hotel, including one from the Duke of Edinburgh. And the village was quiet, very quiet.

An investigation team began to meet at the Sun, and in the bungalow which Donald had rented. Norman Buckley, Ken Norris, Andrew Brown and Mr John Stollery, of the aerodynam-

Clive Glynn, Campbell's apprentice engineer, after the accident, carrying a section of the hull *(Paul Allonby)*

ics department of the Imperial College of Science. Mr Stollery let it be known that he felt confident that nothing about *Bluebird's* shape or design had contributed to the accident.

I told Leo Villa later of my concern about the damage caused by the duck to the spar; he assured me that this could have had no bearing on the crash. As far as *Bluebird* was concerned, streamlining in its accepted sense had no part in the design of her spars, and he reminded me that it was the outer sheathing of the spars which sustained damage – not the square section rigid construction beneath.

Norris asked for any amateur film or still picture of the crash, which might help to show surface conditions at the time of the run, and they were carefully studied to see if they would reveal any clue. Studying enlargements of certain pictures, Norris

The Royal Navy divers preparing their equipment. On the left are Bill Jordan of the RAC and PC Jim Sherdley in the dory *(Paul Allonby)*

noticed ripples on the water, in a shot showing *Bluebird* at speed with her starboard sponson clear of the water.

"These," he said, "look like the wash of the first run, reflected off the bank. If Don hit them on the return run they could have caused the tramping. But I am sure he was in trouble before that – soon after he entered the measured kilometre."

The Royal Navy expressed a wish to have the wreckage salvaged, so that any hydrodynamic factors which might have contributed to the crash could be examined. The wreckage, however, was now the responsibility of the executors of Donald's estate and any decision about salvaging the boat could only be made by them.

The grim search by the divers continued, each of the team making one dive per day, and each dive of a duration of half an hour. This allowed them a total of fourteen minutes on the bed of the lake, working in three feet of fine silt which clouded the water as they moved.

What, to the watchers on the shore, seemed to be a horrible task, was apparently nothing to these men. They had done far worse jobs, under much grimmer conditions. Their usual task was the disposal of bombs and mines found beneath the surface of the seas and, only a few months ago, they had been working in the North Sea, searching for the German submarine which sank there. This present job, diving in the waters of an English lake, they took in their stride, regarding it as an 'exercise'.

As small pieces of wreckage were found, they were brought to the shore and there some of them were broken up into smaller pieces and taken as souvenirs by any who wanted them.

The road around the eastern shore of the lake was sealed off by the police and only those connected with the search, or those known to have been with the project, were permitted to drive to the scene of the search.

We would stand in a quiet group each morning; police, press and members of the *Bluebird* team, and we would watch the progress of the divers. We looked at the lake which, ever since the moment of disaster, had remained absolutely still and mirror-like – and none of us spoke about it.

Andrew Brown and Norman Buckley would visit the scene each morning, stroll slowly along the beach, and look across at the spot where their friend had died. Then they would return to the village to continue the investigation.

Eventually, the forward portion of the wreckage was discovered, lying some 300 feet north of the main hull.

We learned that the cockpit had been completely smashed. The twisted steering wheel and steering column were brought to the surface, and then the harness with which Donald had been

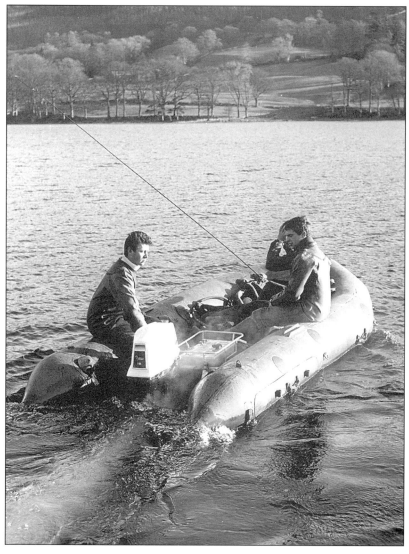

The divers set out from the landing stage to begin their search *(Paul Allonby)*

strapped in his seat was discovered, still in the locked position. The bolts which had secured it into the bulkhead had torn clean through the metal.

Still, there was neither sign nor trace of the body.

Just as a decision was about to be made, calling off the search, Leo Villa, Maurice Parfitt and Lieutenant Commander Futcher visited the ITV studios in Carlisle. There they studied, frame by frame, a film of the tragedy. They believed that an object, seen flying through the air, and emerging from a cloud of spray, could be the body of Donald Campbell; working on the theory that it could have been catapulted two hundred feet north of where the boat crashed, Futcher arranged for the search to be renewed in a different position. However, although bearings were taken from the positions of the cameraman on to trees and other objects on the far shore, and although two schoolboys were taken to the diving area to pinpoint the spot where they said they had seen the body hit the water, not a trace was found.

The police and local residents thought that a body would come to the surface of the lake in nine to thirteen days, so the diving search was then called off, the team returned to Rosyth, and a day-to-day search of the shoreline was commenced; a shoreline still dotted with the small polythene buoyancy bags which came from *Bluebird's* engine compartment.

The investigations continued. The theories abounded. And there was much talk of the 'angle of incidence', the amount of lift to her sponsors which *Bluebird* would tolerate before leaving the water and taking to the air. Donald, we were told, knew that this tolerance amounted to only five or six degrees, that this was the permissible margin between planing on the water and flying through the air, and – knowing this – had gone on, had taken the risk to get his record, to get ahead of the Americans, and to give Britain a 'shot in the arm'.

For Leo Villa assured us that Donald Campbell was a 'patriotic boy' and that he had refused American sponsorship – offered on the condition that he attempted the record in America – in order to gain it in his own country, on Coniston Water.

Perhaps Harry Griffin writing an appreciation of Donald Campbell which was published in the *Lancashire Evening Post* on January 5th expressed it best, when he said:

"Donald Campbell, a cavalier of the jet age who chose to live out on the very edge of life, died in the very moment of his greatest triumph because he pushed his luck just a little too far.

"He had told the world he was adventuring for Britain, and he was indeed, a great patriot, but he really went on and on to the almost inevitable end, because he had no choice."

On Tuesday evening, January 10th, the villagers of Coniston

began to walk through the snow, over the humpbacked bridge, down the main street, until they reached the old church of St Andrew. Headlight beams flickered on the fell slopes approaching the village, as cars bringing people from farther afield approached. A group from the Sun Hotel walked slowly down the hill. When the bell commenced to toll at seven o'clock, the little church was packed to the doors.

Leo Villa and his wife; Maurice Parfitt and the other members of the *Bluebird* team; Lieutenant Commander the Hon. Greville Howard, representing the Campbell family; Norman Buckley and Andrew Brown; pressmen; Dr Darbishire; and representatives of the Windermere Motorboat Racing Club, of which Donald had been a member; police officers and members of the local fire brigade. All came to join with the villagers in paying their last respects and their tribute to Donald Campbell.

The lesson, *"And I saw a new heaven and a new earth ..."* was read by Norman Buckley, Donald's close friend for so many years; and the vicar, the Rev. John Hancock, in his address said:

"Donald Campbell was a man of determination who had surmounted delays and difficulties which must have been tiresome. He was courageous, but knew what he was undertaking and took no irresponsible decisions. He was a great patriot, and believed in the potential of Britain – that there was nothing the country could not achieve if she put her mind to it. It was in demonstrating this belief that he lost his life."

The congregation knelt and sang Donald Campbell's favourite hymn, *"God be in my head and in my understanding."*

*   *   *   *

Those of us who – because of our nine-week association with it – considered ourselves to be part of the Campbell project, and had watched Donald surmounting the snags and frustrations, and had been the recipients of his grins and winks – went our different ways. The *Bluebird* team, the technicians, the photographers, the television crews and the journalists, all, soon after the church service, left Coniston to seek other work, fresh news and new subjects for their camera shutters.

The surface of Coniston Water remained still, reflecting the ridge line of fells with its mantle of snow. The gulls and the wild duck had the lake to themselves once again. Near the timekeepers' wooden platform, a stick from one of the rockets fired on January 4th floated idly.

When, on my way home after my last visit to Coniston, I stopped at the viewpoint, I saw that the lake had become once more a place for fishermen and wild birds. The only trace of the drama which had been enacted there was a small rubber buoy, bobbing about far down the lake.

Two days later, Norman Buckley told us of a pact which had been made between Donald Campbell and himself. He revealed that, after he had gained the world three-hour record in *Miss Windermere* in the spring of 1966, Donald attended a celebration party afterwards. He told Buckley of his intention to attempt a world record of 300 miles per hour. Between them they then planned that once Donald had achieved this, then his friend, again in *Bluebird*, would attempt to become the first man to cover 150 miles in one hour. They were well aware that *Bluebird* had only a relatively small fuel tank to cope with the engine's prodigious thirst, but they felt that refuelling problems could be overcome. Unfortunately, as Donald was announcing publicly his intention of trying for 300 mph, Norman Buckley suffered a heart attack, so his share in the planned 'double' had to be dropped.

On January 18th the *Daily Express* published what they called a 'technological analysis' of *Bluebird's* last two runs. It was done at their instigation and with the co-operation of Royal Air Force photographic experts. The conclusions at which they arrived suggested that, on the first run, it was possible that the boat was travelling at 300 mph. On the approach to the first marker buoy on the second run, 'the boat reached a peak of 328 mph, then for some reason, the speed dropped to 300 mph as it passed the buoy. By the time it took to the air, they suggested *Bluebird* was travelling at about 290 mph.

They developed their theories to a point which suggested that the boat struck a submerged object below the surface, and described how Ken Norris had shown them the starboard planing fin, a piece of stainless steel ground to a sharp edge on its front end. In it were two large indentations which could only have been caused by its striking a piece of driftwood. This impact, they said, would cause the starboard sponson to dip, that its natural buoyancy would bring it back into the air, and there it would stay, making the boat unmanageable. Thus, when just a hundred and fifty yards from the end of the measured kilometre, the boat met the wash of its first run, the port sponson too, would lift, and the critical angle of six degrees would be exceeded.

Donald Campbell, they said, was not out on a do or die mission and when *Bluebird* took off and flipped over on to her back, she was actually slowing.

This will not, however, be the final analysis. Other theories will be propounded and examined for years to come.

And it will not be the end of Donald Campbell's work. Innes Ireland, the racing driver, announced his intention of seeking backers for the building of a new boat, saying that he was willing to take over where Campbell had left off.

"Failure to do so," he said, "would be a tragic waste."

An hotel-keeper in Yorkshire started to raise a fund towards the cost of building a new *Bluebird* and, across in the United States, Craig Breedlove, the man who had beaten Donald's land speed record by using a jet powered engine, and who had described him as 'formidable competition', prepared for his own coming attempt on the world water speed record.

Nineteen days after the tragedy, Lady Campbell was taken out to the buoy in the centre of the lake and to it she tied a small bunch of tulips and irises, in Donald's racing colours.

16

Some of his Friends

WHILE an all party motion was being tabled in the House of Commons and, sponsored by six Members, received very wide support – it asked for public recognition of Donald Campbell's "sustained, courageous and successful endeavours in attaining the world land and water speed records for Britain" – the people of the little Lakeland village of Coniston, who had known the Campbells so well, quietly began to discuss plans for their own personal memorial to Donald and to consider what form it should take. Perhaps a memorial or a seat made from local stone at the northern end of the lake, which affords a view of almost its entire length. Or a plaque, perhaps, somewhere in the village itself. Or something for the children. One day a decision as to form and location will be made. There will be no undue hurrying for there is no need for haste, and when the decision is made, it will not be by some planning board in some distant town, but by the people of Coniston. For this will be their memorial.[1]

Many others, in all walks of life, paid their personal tributes to Donald Campbell.

The Marquis of Bristol, in a letter to *The Times*, indicated that he had been with Donald before his project commenced. I asked him if he would be kind enough to elaborate on this for me and he told me the following:

"It was touch and go whether Donald took the hydro-plane *Bluebird* to Coniston. He had just successfully developed a new type of high-speed family runabout able to sell at a low price. He asked what he should do: pursue his business career, he was on the threshold of success, or try again for the record. I tried to

---

1

A memorial has since been erected: see page 190

dissuade him from trying again, but he said that, although I was quite right, he wished to put it up to three hundred miles per hour, where it would take someone else, starting from scratch, twenty years to catch up.

"My feelings after Coniston were that it was not only the loss of a gallant friend, but the waste of a life of such a person who was undoubtedly one of the best products of this country."

I heard many stories about Donald Campbell from his friends, stories which have no headline value, but help to paint a picture of the man in relaxed mood, away from the spotlight. Friends like Mrs Connie Robinson of the Sun hotel, with whom he stayed so many times.

"I remember so many things about him – so many I wouldn't know where to begin. He had been with us so often, you know, that he really became like one of the family. Like his mother, and his sister Jean, he would come and sit around for hours just chatting with us. They all would, and we discussed everything.

"He loved a cosy, 'homely' atmosphere. His job and his work involved him with so much 'top brass' and took him into such 'high places', but he was never really happy unless he was messing about in sweater and old slacks. He and my son Tony were like brothers; and they would spend hours taking a radio set to pieces and putting it all together again – and getting it to work.

"Perhaps my happiest memory is that of the Christmas he spent with us last year. Everyone had gone home, you know, and Tonia wasn't able to be with him – she was working in cabaret in Bristol – and we all thought he would be lonely. Not a bit of it, though. Very naughtily, he and a few local friends launched *Bluebird* on Christmas morning and he had a run – they had no right to do that, you know – and then he came back to join us for Christmas dinner. We all pulled crackers and exchanged small gifts. We gave him a butcher's apron, blue with white stripes, and with a large pocket. When he found a teddy bear in the pocket, wearing a 'pinny', we told him it was a mate for Mr Whoppit, that this was Mrs Whoppit.

"He would walk into the kitchen and pinch a cold sausage off a plate, or anything else interesting and edible which happened to be there."

Andrew Brown reminded me that in the early days, when Donald's father ran a flourishing motor business in the south, he would have a small silver and blue Saint Christopher medallion screwed to the dashboard of each car he sold, just as a modern car dealer will affix a transfer bearing his name.

"During Donald's stay in Coniston," Andrew continued, "he opened his mail one morning and found a small cardboard box in which someone had sent him one of these medallions. He was most appreciative and very touched.

"I have a framed photograph of Donald at home, on which he wrote: *To Andrew, Companion in many a battle, May his shadow never grow less. In appreciation.* I am proud to think I was with him on his last battle."

And Harry Griffin, the man who had said that record attempts were 'time wasters' and 'a confounded nuisance', but who nevertheless witnessed every one of Donald's attempts in this country, had this to say: "I was setting off on a climbing exercise on one of the crags some years ago. Donald was up here on one of his attempts and I asked him if he would like to join me for the day.

"'Harry, old boy,' he said, 'I'd be scared stiff.'

"Yet Donald, in the matter of sport, was an absolute 'natural'. You know, he learned to water-ski on Coniston Water in just one hour.

"Just after Christmas, only a few days before he attempted the record, I was setting off to do a bit of snow-skiing on High Raise. It was obvious that the weather wasn't going to allow Donald to take *Bluebird* out and he suggested that he would like to come with me. I immediately offered to lend him some skis and equipment, and he was on the point of coming along when he paused, and said, 'This is damned silly, you know, Harry – I might just go and break my bloody ankle or something.'

An early version of *Bluebird* had a double cockpit – one for the driver and one for the engineer. On one occasion Donald took Harry on a high-speed trial in place of Leo Villa, who wanted to observe *Bluebird* from the shore. At the time, the world record was just over 140 mph and they reached 120 mph. Harry was the only journalist to have travelled in *Bluebird* and, for a short time, was the eighth fastest man in the world on water. He later described it as an exciting but frightening experience.

Postscript

On Saturday 28th January, 1967, it was announced in the *London Gazette* that Donald Campbell had been awarded the Queen's Commendation for Gallantry 'for his courage and determination in attacking the world water speed record'. There was a widespread feeling that this award fell short of what Campbell's efforts deserved. Sir Ivan de la Bere, a former Secretary of the Central Chancery of the Orders of Knighthood, explained the situation in a letter to the *Daily Telegraph*. He referred to what people considered the 'quite inadequate recognition' of Campbell's gallant attempts, and continued:

"Unfortunately, under existing rules, his actions, though very brave, did not include the life-saving of others and so could not be rewarded by the George Cross or the Albert Medal, which are the two highest honours available as posthumous gifts for brave civilians."

It has since been announced that a Fellowship will be set up at Imperial College, London University, which will bear the name of Donald Campbell and will encourage research in aerodynamics, the work for which he gave his life. The announcement of the Fellowship was signed by Mr Leo Villa, Sir Max Aitken, Sir Billy Butlin, Lord Camden, Mr William Coley, Mr Charles Forte, Mr Greville Howard, Mr Ralph Loosemore, Mr Victor Mishcon, and the Duke of Richmond and Gordon.

17

World records attained by Donald M. Campbell CBE

Bluebird: Car

Lake Eyre, 1964   403.1 mph

Bluebird: Boat

Ullswater, 1955	202.32 mph
Lake Mead, 1955	216.20 mph
Coniston Water, 1956	225.63 mph
Coniston Water, 1957	239.07 mph
Coniston Water, 1958	248.62 mph
Coniston Water, 1959	260.35 mph
Lake Dumbleyung, 1964	276.33 mph

Speeds attained on Coniston Water 1966-67 during attempts to raise the world record to 300 mph

25th November, 1966	100-120 mph
10th December, 1966	196-202 mph
12th December, 1966	238-261 mph
13th December, 1966	262-267 mph
25th December, 1966	250 mph plus (unobserved)
27th December, 1966	280 mph plus (unobserved)
4th January, 1967	297-300 mph plus

Opposite: the replica of *Bluebird* K7 that was used in the BBC film "Across the Lake", and that is now on view at the Lakeland Motor Museum

Part Three

After Coniston

Graham Beech

18

Mission in Coniston: Raising K7

Sunday 28 January 2001: just over 34 years after Donald Campbell's boat *Bluebird* sank in a welter of spray to the bottom of Coniston Water, a diver was pulled unconscious from the lake. Ironically, he had been injured in only two metres of water whilst untangling a rope after completing a successful dive to 150 feet. A call was made to the ambulance service and the paramedics were on their way. Fog swirled around the village of Coniston, but the diver was quickly recovered to the boat, oxygen administered and he was taken to hospital, where he stayed for three days. Thankfully, he made a full recovery.

Fortunate for the diver but unlucky for the "Bluebird Team" whose cover was now blown. For over four years, this team of dedicated enthusiasts and advanced technical divers had tried to conceal the location of the wreck. The team was led by Bill Smith, managing director of Kiltech Underwater – an offshoot of Bill's vehicle security company in Tyne & Wear. Bill stated that, at first, there was no thought of raising K7. By keeping the location secret, it was said that the team had hoped to walk away at the end of the job, confident that souvenir hunters would be unable to steal parts of *Bluebird*. But a BBC TV documentary was being made, so secrecy would surely be short-lived.

Inevitably, news of the incident with the diver quickly spread and was soon picked up by *The Sunday Telegraph*. On Sunday 4th February 2001 their reporter, Daniel Foggo, revealed plans to salvage *Bluebird* from a depth of nearly 150 ft. Such plans were indeed being discussed by the survey team, BBC TV and some members of the Campbell family. Bill felt that the newspaper story, rather than getting at the truth surrounding the possible salvaging of the boat, sensationalised the alleged personal differences between the various parties. *The Sunday Times* ran a story that Bill felt was nearer the truth, but the damage was done. And so, that Sunday evening, BBC TV News showed us an underwater picture of *Bluebird's* tail fin, still blue after all these years – its Union Flag (upside down on the starboard side) having been carefully cleaned by a diver. By Monday morning, the entire nation knew the story – it was in *The Daily Mail*, *The Daily Express* and *The Guardian*. Plans needed to be reconsidered.

Bill Smith on board the survey boat, *Predator* (by permission of *The Westmorland Gazette*)

Local people

Many local people already knew about Bill Smith's project and, although they were initially and understandably suspicious of the strangers, they showed a keen interest in their activities. They were always willing to have a friendly chat about *Bluebird* and Donald Campbell, their local hero. But, following *The Sunday Telegraph* story, there was a sharp division of opinion on the wisdom of the operation. John Hurst, a local newspaper editor who recalls *Bluebird* being unveiled for the first time wrote, "Let the brave man and his spectacular boat rest in peace in Coniston. Remember *Bluebird* for all her grace and glory." Harry Griffin, veteran climber and the reporter who first broke the news of the tragic accident, described the whole affair as "Quite appalling". Many of the villagers remained against it and Mike Humphreys, custodian of the Ruskin Museum in Coniston, was reported as saying, "It would be wrong to make commercial gain" – but a significant part of Coniston's trade is fuelled one way or another by the Campbell legend and those of its other heroes, living or dead. There was also talk of finding the remains of Donald Campbell, though David Coxon of the Coniston Boating Centre expressed his dismay: "I'm not convinced that trying to get Donald out is the best thing to be done."

These reactions were understandable. For 34 years *Bluebird* had rested peacefully on the bottom of Coniston Water as a silent memorial to a great man, whilst the people of the Lake District, and of Coniston in particular, had been the guardians of his story. But over the intervening years, there have been many important changes. Today's underwater explorers and divers are pushing back the frontiers of their chosen craft with frightening speed. If the equipment used by present-day divers had been available to the Navy in 1967, they would have finished their work in a few days. It was inevitable that someone would go looking for the wreck. Just as it was for the mighty *Titanic*, *Bluebird*'s time would come to be explored again, and when it did, Bill Smith claimed that she might not have been treated with the respect that she rightly deserved. Unfortunately, these good intentions became entwined in Campbell family relationships and the making of a TV programme.

The Family

The operation might have proceeded more smoothly if all members of the Campbell family had been involved and had been in agreement from the start. Unfortunately, this was not the case. Donald's daughter Gina learned of the project and became involved in discussions about plans to locate and film the wreck. Also, Bill Smith met with Don Wales, godson and nephew of Donald Campbell in January 1997 at the Speed Record Club annual dinner to commemorate the 30th anniversary of Donald's death. Don was not particularly enthusiastic about divers visiting the wreck site but it had not been relocated at that stage, so there seemed little to worry about.

Extraordinarily, however, nobody chose to inform Tonia Bern-Campbell, Donald's third wife, then 64 years old and living near to Los Angeles. She only learned of the diving activities in 2001 – allegedly from *The Sunday Telegraph*. Her reaction was initially one of sadness. When she learned of plans to raise *Bluebird*, she was reported as saying "They can't do this without my permission. I have not given it". She had always expressed the wish that the wreck should remain on the lakebed as a memorial to her husband, citing his wish that "The craft stays with the skipper". Bill frankly admits that the fact that she was not told was his fault – it was easy to assume that news would somehow make its way to her over the four years that the team was at work. Tonia was contacted directly by Bill who apologised on behalf of the team for this misunderstanding. She realised that, sooner or later, *Bluebird* would be brought to the surface and therefore had no choice but to give her approval.

Mission almost impossible

As early as 1998, Mike Rossiter, a BBC TV producer, had approached Bill's 'Bluebird Team' with a view to obtaining footage of the *Bluebird* wreck, but that was before it had been relocated. By the time it had been located and the debris field mapped, the project had become fascinating in its own right. So, a deal was struck to film a re-enactment of the discovery of *Bluebird* for a full-scale BBC TV documentary, initially thought to be in a series called 'The Mission' but eventually broadcast on 7th June, 2001 as 'A British Legend: The Search for *Bluebird*'. From October 2000, Mike Rossiter's film crew was based at Anthony Robinson's Coniston Lodge Hotel and Bluebird Team divers made regular sorties in Coniston Water. It was then that the possibility of raising the wreck was first seriously considered. Gina visited the team and the question of preserving the wreck properly was discussed.

In an unconscious echo of January 1967, time was seen to be precious – winter was closing in and weather conditions were worsening. Secrecy was everything. Inquiries about the programme from journalists were ignored. Telephone calls were never returned. The divers – and

Mike Rossiter, BBC producer
(photo by Jeff Morris, the Daily Mail)

others – were asked to sign confidentiality agreements. Eventually, it reached the stage where nobody knew who else was supposed to know – but Coniston is a small place and rumours continued to spread. Perhaps if the BBC and others had taken responsible writers into their confidence, there would have been more accurate reporting and less possibility of allegedly false rumours.

After the report in *The Sunday Telegraph*, however, it was too late to consider leaving the wreck where it was. It was claimed that knowledgeable divers could soon work out its location and it would be only a matter of time before *Bluebird* was dismantled piece by piece, leaving behind, at the most, its skeleton. So, the operation proceeded. Parts of the shattered forward section were brought to the surface bit-by-bit and stored away from the gaze of curious onlookers, though Bill Smith delayed the actual raising of the main, stern section until he had obtained permission from Gina. "It's Gina's boat," he said. "It's entirely up to her."

But was this the case? On February 7th a new problem arose: Paul Foulkes-Halbard of Filching Manor near Eastbourne (see page 192) already owned substantial quantities of Campbell memorabilia and reasserted his claim as the legal owner of the wreck. The BBC were advised of this, but their response was that it was up to Paul to pursue his claim against "the combined might of the Campbells". The area of ownership became as murky as the silty lakebed of Coniston Water. Both Donald and *Bluebird* had been insured and one story was that insurance had been offered in lieu of sponsorship – having been an insurance broker, he had contacts in the insurance industry, so this was possible. Although details of the policies and settlement seemed hazy, it is known that the insurers *did* pay out. However, marine insurers, having paid up, are not required to take possession and are free to "wash their hands" of a wreck, to avoid subsequent liability such as pollution from leaking fuel. It was claimed that, in this case, they followed the Campbell family's wishes by renouncing any claim and agreeing that it should be left undisturbed as a grave. Exactly who owned the wreck became the subject of a legal wrangle between Foulkes-Halbard and the Campbell estate. If Foulkes-Halbard owned it, where was the proof? Even if the wreck had been sold to a third party, some began to wonder if, since it had been on the lakebed for so long, might it be argued that ownership would have reverted to the

Campbell estate or to the owners of the lake bed – the Rawdon-Smith trust.

By February 9th members of the family appeared to have settled any differences that may have existed between themselves. Don Wales dismissed stories of a rift, saying, "There's no family row ... it's just not true." He admitted that local feeling was initially that the boat should have stayed at the bottom of the lake, but that events had forced their hand. Don became the spokesman for Gina, Tonia and his mother, Jean, Donald's sister. He expressed their desire for a dignified occasion when *Bluebird* was brought out of the lake, saying "We want to pay our respects to our relation privately rather than in the full glare of the media". That was not to be the case, however.

Technology and the Bluebird Team

The *Sunday Telegraph* report seemed like such bad luck for all concerned – but just how much of a mystery was the location of the wreck? It was no mystery at all at the time of the crash because, soon after *Bluebird* sank, Royal Navy divers had located the wreckage and brought various sections to the surface – so they certainly knew where it was.

Robin Brown, chairman of the K7 Club at the time of the 2000/2001 recovery operation, was one person who had always been reasonably certain of *Bluebird*'s location. Immediately after the crash, Robin was involved in searching the surface of the lake for any sign of Donald and, though unsuccessful, he helped to construct an exact plan that showed exactly where *Bluebird* was lying. A marker buoy was even placed to mark the location of the wreck but, as time passed, it was realised that opportunist divers might go 'trophy hunting' – so the buoy was removed and knowledge of *Bluebird's* position started to become less precise.

After 34 years, it was not a simple matter to get back to the scene of the accident. In theory, it should have been because it was filmed and photographed at the time, and there was the plan that had been drawn by Robin Brown. There were eyewitnesses who tried to help Bill Smith's team pinpoint the location, but their memories were dulled by the passage of time and there were virtually no permanent visual references on the shore except for a few trees – and these are living things, they grow and die. A fresh approach was needed.

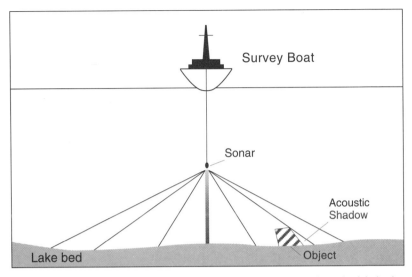

Side-scan sonar: sound waves travel from the instrument at an angle to the lakebed. The strength of the sound echo is converted into shades of grey: hard objects are rendered as white, very soft material as black.

So, it was back to basics and the application of an underwater survey that assumed no knowledge of where the wreck lay. Credit for the rediscovery of *Bluebird* and its subsequent recovery certainly goes to Bill Smith. His passion is to explore wrecks and he has several remarkable missions to his credit, which he plans to chronicle in book form. So far as *Bluebird* was concerned, he had a considerable advantage over other amateur divers who had tried to locate the wreck because they were hampered by inaccurate information and by the murky conditions on the silt-laden lakebed. Bill had previously used state-of-the-art technology in some of his other projects, including powerful acoustic imaging systems such as side-scan sonar. This uses a sonar array towed by a boat on the end of a long cable (see opposite page) to produce images by firing sound waves through the water. A powerful computer then builds an image of the lake bed either side of the vessel. Scanning sonar was also employed; this uses a similar principle but it sits on a tripod on the lake bed and looks around itself, the resulting acoustic image being similar to that which is seen on a radar screen.

Acoustic imaging is ideal for obtaining a vague view of a submerged object in murky conditions, such as exist at the bottom of Coniston Water. But when objects have been located,

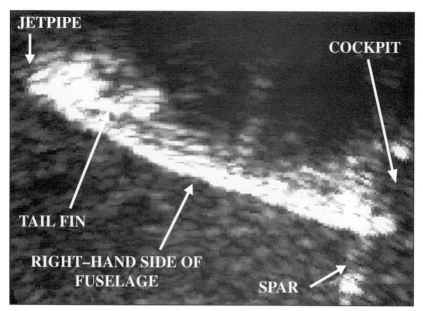

JETPIPE

COCKPIT

TAIL FIN

RIGHT–HAND SIDE OF
FUSELAGE   SPAR

Sector-scan acoustic image of *Bluebird* lying at the bottom of Coniston Water.
(Reproduced with thanks to Bill Smith of the Bluebird Project)

Remotely Operated Vehicles (ROVs) are sent down for a look. These are small, swimming robots with thrusters, cameras and lights. They move in to gather video footage without the disturbance caused by divers and without anyone having risked their lives. Very precise details about objects on the bottom of the lake can be gathered in this way.

Bill's team surveyed the crash site over a period of four years using this equipment and developed the necessary techniques to allow them to locate, identify and recover very small objects in deep water. This is what Kiltech Underwater set out to learn and the *Bluebird* wreck site was a perfect place to practice. It represented a genuine undisturbed and mostly unexplored wreck site.

In August 2000, Bill located the main wreck simply by diving where he thought the wreck should be. At the bottom of the lake his head light failed and he was relying on a hand-held torch. As luck would have it, his foot hooked around a piece of metal and when he turned around to look, he saw the top of *Bluebird*'s fuselage. "Everywhere was blue" said Bill. He looked around and saw pieces of the smashed cockpit, and realised how violent the crash must have been. But, at last there was a success to report to his team aboard their boat, *Predator*.

The Salvage Operation

During February, a pair of barges arrived in the car park by the Bluebird Café – the Bluebird Team's favoured refereshment place. Ostensibly there for routine lake maintenance, their real purpose soon became clear as they were equipped with cranes and salvage equipment. On Friday 2nd March, they were assembled into a floating platform from which to retrieve *Bluebird*, two miles down the lake. Once in position, concrete blocks were placed around the wreck and the platform anchored to them.

On Saturday 3rd March, divers attached strops to the outriggers at the front of the wreck. Next day, after fitting further strops to the stern, lifting cables were attached and the crane on the barge was used to lift *Bluebird*'s front end clear of the silt. After two days of technical problems, *Bluebird* was prised from the lakebed on Wednesday 7th March. She was raised to the surface five metres at a time by the use of air-filled lift bags on the lifting cables until she was resting just five metres below the surface.

Very early on the morning of Thursday 8th March, the barge was released from its concrete anchors and it began towing *Bluebird* on her two-mile journey to the northern end of the lake. I was also travelling north – but on the M6 – and, just before 8am, I arrived in Coniston with early-morning sunshine. The day before, I'd been tipped off that *Bluebird* was to be brought out of the lake today, not on Sunday as we had been told. This would disappoint many, but potential crowd problems and a worsening foot-and-mouth epidemic were blamed – though it may also have had something to do with conflicting TV schedules. But word had inevitably got around. As I drove down Lake Road towards the Bluebird Café, "no parking" signs were everywhere. No cars were allowed near the lake, so it was back to the village and a long walk back to where the action was.

Attempts at secrecy had failed again – they always do. A media circus was in full swing by the time I returned. Sky TV were there, with a van bearing twin satellite dishes for live coverage. And BBC TV, Granada and all the national newspapers including the *Mail on Sunday*. After a quick coffee and a bacon sandwich I joined the throng, already a hundred or so, clustered around the lakeside and the jetty to where *Bluebird* would be dragged ashore. The sunshine became more hesitant, with clouds on the fells forecasting a change.

Soon after 8am the barge, used as a floating operations platform was on the move towards the jetty. By around 8.30 it was stationary. Divers were in the water and we got a cheery wave from Bill Smith. Four flotation bags, each able to support 500kg, were visible. These were used to support *Bluebird* for the final positioning of the craft. Work then proceeded slowly and delicately – we were told "another hour".... "just another hour".

It was 10.30am before we saw *Bluebird*'s blue tail fin, poking up between the flotation bags. We also saw Tonia Bern-Campbell aboard the barge witnessing the dramatic view of her husband's boat now coming to the surface of the lake, surrounded by the Lakeland fells that he loved. As if to emphasise the drama, the temperature fell, clouds came in and a few drops of rain were felt. Though huddled together, by now we were all feeling the effects of the chilling weather and were willing the team to get on with the job.

Tonia left the barge, came back to the jetty and walked back to the little "Wendy House" of the Coniston Boating Centre. No sign of Gina, but a feisty media person with Tonia was said to be fending off potential questioners – we learned that the *Mail on Sunday* had, according to the BBC reporter standing next to me, signed an exclusive deal for her side of the story. So no interviews, not even for BBC TV, though in newspaper reports the next day she was quoted as saying to Ken Norris, "It has helped to lay the past to rest".

11.30. More delays. The crane on the barge was helping to manoeuvre the 1½ ton hulk over a trailer that was already in the lake and attached by a hawser to the winch of a Landrover parked on the shore. Everything had to

Tonia Bern-Campbell with, right, Anthony Robinson *(photo by Jeff Morris, the Daily Mail)*

"It was 10.30am before we saw *Bluebird*'s blue tail fin,
poking up between the flotation bags." *(Graham Beech)*

be just perfect to avoid damage to the boat: *Bluebird* was
suspended over the trailer and then, around noon, the airbags
were deflated, allowing her to sink precisely into position.

At 12.20 the winch was started and slowly, slowly *Bluebird*
began her final journey to dry land. There was fitful sunshine
and the excitement made us forget the chilling wind. Then, by
12.30 with Bill Smith riding on her stern, *Bluebird* was beached.
And what a sorry sight she was. Only the rear section had
survived and there was a large dent between the tail fin and the
main body. But the horror of it all was to see the bulkhead behind
the cockpit – as wrecked and crumpled as if a bomb had caused
the damage. Yet the paintwork was still sapphire blue after all
these years. The wreckage was checked by the police for any
signs of Campbell's body and a local vicar was on standby, but no
remains were found.

The Bluebird Team was rightly jubilant – a demanding
technical job had been completed without damage to the wreck
and without personal injuries. The cameramen had done their
jobs and the media folk had completed their deals. But some of
us felt that the event could have been more dignified. In *The Mail*

Bluebird alongside the jetty – safely recovered from the depths of Coniston Water *(Graham Beech)*

Tonia Bern-Campbell, seen through the wreckage of *Bluebird* *(photo by Jeff Morris, the Daily Mail)*

on Sunday of 11th March, Tonia was reported as saying "I didn't think it would be an Easter Parade" – referring to what seemed to be the light-hearted tone adopted by Bill with his trademark dragon's tail hat and cheery thumbs-up.

Thoughts of making this crumpled heap of metal into a macabre tourist attraction could surely not be entertained by anybody with respect for Donald Campbell. But stranger things have happened. After the wreck had been recovered, it was sprayed with wax, wrapped in polythene and transported to Tyneside where restoration began. But to what stage? A cleaned-up wreck with its missing bits, including the sponsons, replaced by wooden prostheses? And as a tourist attraction?

A Future for Bluebird?

To the casual observer, it might seem hard to imagine what tangible benefits have resulted from raising *Bluebird*. The TV programme had been made, the skills of Bill Smith's team had been demonstrated and preservation of the wreck had begun. There was the possibility of displaying a restored *Bluebird* in some public place – it was possible that she had potential as an educational tool, from a historical point of view, and for students of engineering, aerodynamics, hydrodynamics, metallurgy, artefact preservation and many other disciplines.

Except for its main steel frame, the other materials of K7 were of aluminium alloy, so no corrosion of these should have occurred, especially since the oxygen content is minimal at such a depth of water. The wreck has been examined for clues to the possible causes of the accident, which could be of vital importance in the design of future boats, including *Quicksilver* KX, in which Nigel Macknight plans to tackle the speed record. Within days of the recovery of the wreck, Ken Norris, 79-year-old designer of K7, started to examine *Bluebird* and found that the water brake was in the 'down' position – see page 187 for the significance of this finding. Also, it was important to examine the fuel tank to try to prove whether or not *Bluebird* ran out of fuel mid-way through her final run – an event that almost certainly would have caused her to flip over, as intimated on page 175. However, during the final stages of the salvage operation, a diver was said to have tasted jet fuel in the water; later, gallons of fuel were drained from the wreck. Shortage of fuel was, therefore, unlikely to have been a major factor.

A final view of *Bluebird* as she was hauled past the Coniston Boating Centre, on the way to possible restoration. Tonia is on the left of the picture. *(Graham Beech)*

Whatever the final result, a complete analysis or reconstruction will not be easy. The sponsors (forward floats) were left floating forlornly on the lake after the crash and were towed back to the boat house by the safety boats. They were then stored in a barn near Haywards Heath, Sussex but were subsequently buried under layers of hardcore and concrete when the barn was demolished and the site developed for industrial purposes. Ken Norris has attempted to locate some items, including the seat, but many of the fragments of the front section, including the cockpit canopy, have been recovered so it might be possible for *Bluebird* to be reconstructed – though to what degree is far from settled.

The Search for Donald

The most puzzling aspect of the *Bluebird* story was that, until May 2001, no part of Donald Campbell's body nor any shred of his clothing had surfaced. His seat, helmet and life-jacket were recovered shortly after the crash, together with his socks, boots and one of his gloves – not as strange as it may seem, since similar losses of clothing ('undressing') have occurred in aviation accidents. His safety harness, which had been bolted to the rear cockpit bulkhead, was, remarkably, still fastened. On later examination, about six inches of the crotch strap of the harness were found to be attached to the anchorage point, either torn by the force of the accident or, more likely, cut through by the Navy divers when they retrieved the harness in 1967. Most of the bolts that had secured the harness to the bulkhead were partially pulled through and one had almost certainly pulled through completely, enabling the body to be released.

Several attempts were made to explain the absence of a body. The most bizarre was that Campbell was not in *Bluebird* on the return run. Attractive as this may be to conspiracy theorists, it would have been highly unlikely to have succeeded with the technology available in 1967, requiring Campbell to have piloted the boat by remote control and to have executed the crash with absolute certainty. Such theories often emerge after the deaths of high-profile personalities – Elvis Presley, John F. Kennedy and Diana, Princess of Wales, being just three examples.

More realistic theories included the body being sucked into the air intake, which seemed improbable in such a severe crash, or that he was trapped against the forward bulkhead – see the side view on page 38. But the Bluebird Team mapped every piece of the shattered cockpit and believed that there was not one single piece big enough to trap a body. After detailed examination of archive film footage and of the wreck, it appears that the tips of both sponsons struck the surface almost simultaneously. The sponsons would have been ripped away first, then the main spar and the cockpit. Campbell's body would probably have been torn from his seat at this point and pushed into the water with a force originally estimated to be as high as 350G. This now seems to have been a considerable over-estimate, but it would still have been massive enough to have expelled all the air from his lungs, causing his body – possibly still largely intact – to sink.

After sinking, a body usually floats back up to the surface as it fills with gas due to decomposition of stomach contents, but the bottom of Coniston Water is cold and deep and decomposition down there is a slow process. Even so, it might be expected that decomposition would eventually have occurred and that only a skeleton would have remained. But this is not necessarily so: a corpse can, under suitable conditions, undergo a process of 'saponification' (literally, 'turning to soap') whereby a waxy, and sometimes hard, substance called *adipocere* is produced by the action of anaerobic bacteria on the fat and soft tissues of a body. In cold, fresh water, adipocere formation can commence within three weeks of death; the resultant waxy layer may completely cover the outline of a body and preserve it by inhibiting the growth of bacteria which would normally digest muscle tissue. If saponification had occurred, it was worthwhile to continue searching for identifiable remains; there was also the hope that if Campbell's one-piece blue overall had remained reasonably intact, everything would have stayed within it. Since no fragment of the overall had ever surfaced, Bill Smith began to believe that Campbell's body was still on the lakebed – and that it had to be within a small area that his team could define.

May 2001: A Body is Found

It was just sheer bad luck that the Navy divers did not find Campbell's body in 1967 – they had completed a systematic search and could have been just inches away. But 34 years later, and with a large area of wreckage to sift through, Bill Smith's team were optimistic that they would succeed. Contrary to the Navy report, the team were convinced that the forces involved were insufficient to cause the body to disintegrate and were hopeful that the remains had been preserved. Hopes were raised in the final week of February, 2001, when rumours circulated about the discovery of a skeleton. Though these were premature, the search continued, with attention directed at the fragments of *Bluebird* strewn along the lakebed after the first point of impact.

Floodlighting, high-resolution sonar and Remotely Operated Vehicles (ROVs) were used to search the lakebed systematically. Success came on Saturday 26th May with an announcement the following Monday by Inspector Paul Coulson, of Cumbria Police: "At approximately 1pm today, partial remains of what is believed to be a human body were recovered from the bed of Coniston Water." A source said to be close to the search team reported the remains to be in 'good condition', adding that there appeared to be some doubt about their completeness. Divers recovered personal effects including a Dunhill lighter inscribed "D.C. Bluebird 403.1mph, July 17th, 1964", a gold St Christopher pendant with the words "To Donald from Daddy, November 1940", a St Christopher keyring, and some coins. He was still wearing his right glove and overalls bearing Union Jacks – open to the waist and revealing a black leather trouser belt.

Gina Campbell, in the presence of Mike Rossiter's BBC TV camera team, expressed her relief, saying: "He can now rest in peace in the right place". She placed two black tulips on a casket that had been draped with a Union Flag when it was brought ashore. As might have been expected, not all of the family welcomed the news. Campbell's sister, 77-year-old Jean Wales, said: "This is the last thing I wanted ... they should let him rest there", while Tonia Bern-Campbell was said by friends to be "too upset" to comment. Many agreed, however, with Robin Brown of the K7 Club: "He deserves a proper funeral and burial ... he was a very brave man who deserves a proper and lasting memorial."

The remains were taken to Barrow-in-Furness general hospital for a post-mortem. DNA samples were taken and compared with those from Gina Campbell and from Jean Wales. Due to the poor quality of samples taken from the remains, identification was an exceedingly slow process. But finally, in a brief hearing on 10th August, the coroner, Ian Smith, was told that the DNA evidence indicated that the remains were 1.9 million times more likely to be those of Donald Campbell than anyone else.

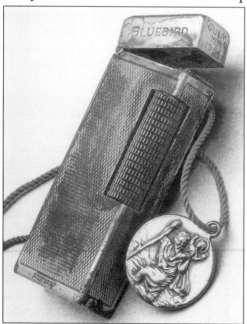

Evidence was also presented by Carl Langhorn of Cumbria Constabulary, relating to the clothing and personal items that had been recovered, which were consistent with what Campbell was wearing on the day of the accident. Satisfied with the identification, the coroner released the remains for burial and adjourned the hearing to a later date to determine the cause of death; further information on the state of the remains may also then be presented.

Donald Campbell's dunhill Rollagas lighter together with his St Christopher medallion *(photograph courtesy of The dunhill Museum & Archive)*

September 2001: The Final Run

Because of his long association with the village, it was appropriate for the funeral of Donald Campbell to take place in Coniston. Tonia, widowed by the fatal crash, said that she would agree to whatever the family wanted, although she would have liked a small private ceremony, followed by a cremation. Gina, his only daughter, had worked for years to preserve her father's achievements and wanted to give him a send-off more worthy of a hero. Announcing her plans for a major public event, she said, "I want it to be a celebration – I want anybody and everybody who feels their lives have been touched by my father to attend".

Gina took on the organisation and funding of the occasion, which would take place on Wednesday, September 12th. I was pleased to be invited to the service, for this would be an opportunity to share in an event that, though tinged with sadness, would be a celebration of Donald Campbell's life and achievements. Inevitably, however, the terrorist attacks of the preceding day on the World Trade Center and The Pentagon cast a long shadow – the civilised world was transfixed by the horror of it all. But despite widespread feelings of shock and foreboding, postponement was not considered appropriate. Quite rightly, the day went ahead as planned, with many hundreds of people preparing to pay tribute to a brave and modest man.

I set out for the Lake District as scheduled at 7am, on a journey with echoes of 8th March – when I followed the same route to witness *Bluebird* being recovered from Coniston Water. After arriving in the village soon after 9am, I again walked down Lake Road to the Bluebird Café, opposite to where *Bluebird* had been winched in, little more than six months earlier. The weather was remarkably similar: an overcast sky with just hints of morning sunshine, though there was an autumnal chill in the air towards the end of a glorious English summer. In normal times, this would also have been the end of a bumper tourist season for the Lake District, but Foot and Mouth had put paid to that.

With a small crowd, I looked out across the steel-grey lake. It was easy to imagine the shriek of a jet engine and the sight of *Bluebird* hurtling across the water. But today there was a strengthening wind and the lake was getting choppier – Campbell would have seen these as unsuitable conditions for record attempts! Inside the café, familiar faces appeared – Bill Smith and members of his diving team, Paul Allonby who had photographed the record attempts, and a clutch of newspaper and TV reporters. Customers were browsing through Campbell memorabilia: from books and limited edition prints to commemorative copies of the funeral service signed by Gina.

Those remaining here would be rewarded with one of the most dramatic and emotional events of the day. At the suggestion of Andy Griffin, a dedicated Campbell enthusiast, Donald Campbell was to be taken across Coniston Water to complete his 'final run' beyond the crash site, after which the coffin would be brought to shore and unloaded at the jetty. But it was 10.30am and I had to return to the village. As I walked back, there was a steady stream of photographers, reporters and local people heading towards the lakeside. Soon, there would be hundreds.

Though a fine drizzle had started, people were already lining the streets, preparing to pay their last respects. I was heading for The Sun hotel – Donald Campbell's headquarters during his daring attempts to push past the 300mph mark. Today it was the venue for Campbell supporters, many of whom I had only known as names on e-mails. As ever, the biggest surprise is to see people in real life: without exception, they are bigger, smaller, older or younger than imagined. Here was Dean Cox of the "Across the Lake" web site, Andy Griffin, who set up the Speed Record discussion group, Mike Varndell of the Bluebird Supporters Club, and many more – comparing notes, looking at old newspaper accounts and admiring photographs of their hero.

There was, however, little time for leisurely mid-morning conversation. Shortly after 11 am, I made my way back to the centre of the village past growing crowds of onlookers who were standing – undeterred – in the heavy rain that had set in. The coffin had, by now, been taken from the hearse and transferred to the *Ruskin* ferry moored at Pier Cottage. The boat, flying a Red Ensign at half mast, sailed down the lake to the crash site where it paused for a few moments while a lone piper played a lament. The 'final run' was then completed and at 12.15pm the coffin, draped in a Union Flag, was transferred to the jetty near the Bluebird Café; from here, it was taken by horse-drawn carriage along Lake Road, for the mile-long journey to St Andrew's Church in Coniston. The cortège was headed by Robin Brown of the K7 Club and Anthony 'Robbie' Robinson, a close friend of Donald. Gina, carrying a bouquet of blue and yellow roses – the colours of *Bluebird* – followed the carriage, linking arms with

Tonia Bern-Campbell. Despite the rain, the route was lined with over 1,000 people, including local schoolchildren waving small flags that they had made.

In the church, the cortège was awaited by 200 members of the congregation. Each had received an order of service illustrated with photographs appropriate to the speed-king's career and containing a replica of the blue-enamelled plates that were attached to the dashboards of the Campbells' cars and boats.

Treasured souvenir: a replica 'Blue Bird' plate

The service, conducted by the Rev. Mark East, began at 1pm to the strains of Gershwin's "Rhapsody in Blue". The coffin was carried by Donald's three nephews, Donald Wales, Malcolm and Peter Hulme and by Bill Smith and two of the other divers who had recovered the body, Carl Spencer and Graham Woodfine. The congregation joined in a few moments of prayer and contemplation for the victims of the terrorist attacks in America, and then the service proceeded as planned, relayed by loudspeakers to the hundreds of people outside the church.

Music for the service had been selected by Gina to complement her father's remarkable life. The K-Shoes Male Voice Choir sang Psalm 121 – 'I will lift up mine eyes unto the hills' – and 'Speed Your Journey' (from Verdi's *Nabucco*). Steve Hogarth, lead singer with rock band Marillion, gave a moving performance of 'Out of This World' – the 1995 song that inspired Bill Smith to begin the search for *Bluebird.*'

Representing the K7 Club, Robin Brown read the Lesson using the text from Ecclesiastes 44 – 'Let us now praise famous men' – and there was a moving, personal tribute by Anthony Robinson who reminded us of the courage it must have taken each time Donald Campbell stepped into the cockpit of his *Bluebird* boat or car. Finally, Nat King Cole's 'Unforgettable' – one of Donald Campbell's favourite songs – completed the eclectic choice of music for this memorable service.

Whilst this was taking place, a service was being held simultaneously on water. Gordon Hall, the owner of Coniston Ferries, provided two of his boats to enable 60 people to pay their last respects near to the crash site. This service was conducted by Canon Danny Sanderson, Rural Dean of Furness.

"Coming Home" – Donald Campbell's last journey on Coniston Water. © Andy Griffin 2001

Back on dry land, but under torrential rain, the cortège and horse-drawn carriage left the church, went along a crowded Tilberthwaite Avenue and to the cemetery in Hawkshead Old Road. Donald Campbell was interred in a grave close to that of Connie Robinson and her family – Connie was the proprietor of The Sun hotel in 1967 – and a temporary marker stone produced by Bowness stonemason Andrew Irvine was unveiled.

The service was followed by afternoon tea at Windermere Motor Boat Racing Club. This was an opportunity to meet people I had come to know during this exceptional year. Gina arrived with Mister Whoppit, Donald's teddy bear mascot; and here also were Don Wales, Bill Smith, Nigel Macknight, Mike Rossiter and many others – all meeting in a common cause. And at last I met Ken Norris, the designer of *Bluebird* – still sprightly, still the enthusiastic engineer ever willing to talk about his creation of half a century ago. And finally Tonia –

The temporary marker stone
(Graham Beech)

with whom I had only ever been in contact by fax. Charming, vivacious and entertaining – she and Donald must, in happier times, have been a stunning couple.

"... the cortège and horse-drawn carriage then left the church, went along a crowded Tilberthwaite Avenue and to the cemetery in Hawkshead Old Road." *(Graham Beech)*

"Donald Campbell was interred in a grave close to that of Connie Robinson ..." Rev. Mark East is followed by Anthony Robinson, left, and Robin Brown *(Phil Evans)*

The Troubled Ownership of Bluebird

From the recovery of *Bluebird* almost to the day of the funeral, there was one major unresolved dispute: Paul Foulkes-Halbard's claim to own the wreckage of *Bluebird*. A car and boat enthusiast with a large collection of Campbell memorabilia, Paul was a friend of Leo Villa and knew several of Campbell's relations. I and others often suggested to Paul that it would surely simplify matters if evidence of his claim, based on papers that he stated to have in his possession, could be put in the public domain. He declined to do so, and consistently stated his ownership of the wreck – though stopping short of demanding that it should be moved permanently to his home at Filching Manor in Sussex.

On 16th May 2001 it was reported that a High Court action had been brought by Mishcon de Reya, solicitors to the estate of Donald Campbell, to establish ownership. A High Court order was obtained, ensuring that the wreckage remained in the workshop of Bill Smith's team in Newcastle-upon-Tyne until the action could be settled. Mishcon de Reya stated that, "Campbell's family, including his widow Tonia, wish the boat to be kept in Coniston, ultimately at the Ruskin Museum".

Events dragged on, with little sign of progress. At the end of June, however, Paul Foulkes-Halbard was admitted to hospital suffering from, it was reported, a minor stroke. This may well have had no bearing on subsequent events but, on 7th September, Mishcon de Reya issued a news release stating that a Consent Order had been lodged with the High Court in London, whereby the Executors of Donald Campbell's estate, Lord Mishcon and Tonia Bern-Campbell, were declared to be the rightful owners of *Bluebird* and that Paul Foulkes-Halbard had relinquished his claim. The news release went on to say that the executors had arranged for *Bluebird* to be transferred to the Campbell Heritage Trust[1] and that the family intended that the boat should be based long-term at the Ruskin Museum in Coniston.

Although Gina appeared, at one stage, to oppose plans to house the boat within an extension to the Ruskin Museum, Mishcon de Reya subsequently stated that "Gina ... does not oppose the plan and is looking at whether the boat could be

---

[1] The trustees include Donald Wales, Gina Campbell, Jean Wales and other immediate family members; the aims of the trust may include protection of the family name, licensing and merchandising rights, and raising money for sponsorship of future speed record attempts.

based at the lakeside, albeit it is not expected that planning permission would be granted ...".

Bluebird might, therefore, be found a final resting place in Coniston. If so, it could provide a marketing opportunity for the museum and a welcome boost for tourism. In the hope that a formal, long-term agreement could be reached with the legal owners of the wreckage, and following discussions with Mishcon de Reya and Donald Wales, the Ruskin Museum submitted, in June 2001, a planning application for a purpose-built extension comprising a 100 sq metre display area linked to the main museum by a 25 sq metre annexe. The Lake District National Park Authority's Development Control Committee met on 2nd August to consider the application and conditional consent was granted on 4th September.

It seems certain, however, that *Bluebird* will be moved from the North-East. Kevin Wheatcroft, a director of the Leicestershire-based Donington Grand Prix Collection, had taken a great interest in the recovery operation; subsequently, a business arrangement was entered into with the Campbell Heritage Trust, whereby *Bluebird* would be taken to Donington, expertly preserved in her current state and then placed on temporary exhibition. For most people, this will be their first opportunity to see the famous record-breaker.

* * * *

This part of the story would be incomplete without a comment from Paul Foulkes-Halbard, who had been left with little alternative but to accept an unconditional Consent Order, renouncing his claim. Paul, who always spared time to give me his views of events as they unfolded, provided the following statement: "After a mature consideration, I decided to agree a Consent Order to the Estate of the late Donald Campbell in respect of the *Bluebird* K7. My reasoning behind this is that I had been persuaded by the Campbell family and the people of Coniston that the right and proper place for the vessel to be exhibited was as near as possible to the body of Donald Campbell". Paul maintained that his motives were 'pure' in that he had been anxious to secure the vessel for Britain, whilst pointing out that K7 had killed Donald Campbell, nearly killed Graham Woodfine, the Bluebird Project diver, and "had a fair chance of killing me".

19

What Really Happened to Bluebird?

T HIS chapter has been compiled directly from text and diagrams supplied by Ken Norris, the designer of *Bluebird* K7 and of the new *Quicksilver* KX. Ken is still very active as a consultant to land and water speed record projects. His memories of the final days in the *Bluebird* project are recorded here, together with his analysis of what went wrong.

Christmas Day, 1966

An excited voice over the telephone – it's Donald Campbell from Coniston: "Great news Ken – two excellent runs today. The new fuel pump has done the trick – plenty of thrust. Water brake tested OK. So come up quickly – I'm calling for the timekeepers."

"Great, Donald I'm on my way!"

Marjorie, my wife, and I pack our bags. With our nine year-old son William and two year-old John (Donald's godson, who was born in 1964 when Donald broke both water speed and land speed records) we speed up to Coniston. We arrive and are met with frustration. Coniston is not a happy lake: its surface is untiring in its frivolity, there is wind and rain day after day. The Old Man of Coniston refused to show his face.

Donald and his team are weary after being there since early November and having to follow their regular routine: up very early in the cold and often miserable mornings, just enough time for toast and coffee at the Sun Hotel in Coniston and then off to the lake in the dark to wait for that magic moment. The moment when the wind drops, the rain clears, the lake says 'OK' and it's all hands on deck at great speed for a trial or record run.

January 3rd, 1967

Frustration continues with the end of the week looming, and the cliff-hangers of record-breaking have prevailed again. The weather forecast is grim. Business and family duties beckon, and I must regretfully return to 'hold the fort'. On the evening of 3rd of January we say goodbye to Donald, who is at Connie's cottage.

"Please stay" says Donald, embracing Marjorie.

"Weather forecast says 'no go' Donald – I'll come back at the end of this week."

There was a quiet, slow response from Donald who looked thoughtful and determined, "Please don't go, it'll be all over in the morning." He was right – but not in the way he expected.

We got into the car and drove back through the night to our home in West Sussex. We had been awake for some 20 hours and my conscience is pricking me – I don't like leaving Donald as we did, Marjorie is feeling the same – should we turn back? My reasoning said no, as the weather dictates that there will be no runs for some days. When it does, we will then return smartly to Coniston and give Donald the support he merits.

January 4th, 1967

We arrived home in the early evening as daylight was disappearing. We unpacked and tried to snatch some sleep. Then, at 08:30 on the 4th January, a telephone call to Marjorie from a friend, Christine Bond, brought us rapidly to our senses.

"Had we heard the dreadful news? A bad accident."

I drove rapidly to my office – Norris Brothers at Haywards Heath. "Was Donald OK?"

"No, I'm afraid he's at the bottom of the lake," said my brother Eric.

There were all sorts of questions as to what happened. My other brother Lewis (Marine Engineer and co-Chief Designer of K7 and CN7) and I make a rapid trip to Coniston to find out – there was no 'nodding off' on this run. My garbled thoughts were screaming at me:

"What on earth went wrong with K7? What happened to Donald? What could go wrong?"

We arrived at Coniston and set about trying to find out what had happened. Many questions were put to the people who saw the accident – Leo Villa, David Benson *(Daily Express)*, Norman Buckley, the timekeepers and many others.

The consensus was that Donald had made a very good run from north to south. He used the water brake to slow down, but uncharacteristically turned and came straight back over the wash of the water brake, without calling on the radio-telephone to establish surface conditions along the lake.

Well into the measured kilometre, K7 took to the air, made an almost complete loop and dived at a steep angle back into the lake. This made the craft roll forward stern over bow, breaking off the floats and rapidly sinking into the lake. No structural damage of the machine took place until it dived in after almost completing its loop into the lake.

Mr Whoppit, the floats and much debris came to the surface. The cockpit seat was recovered with the seatbelt still fastened. Divers were called, but they could not establish where Donald's body was. Possible causes of the accident were discussed but no conclusions could be drawn at the time.

Lew and I collected every bit of data that could help to establish the cause of the accident. With the help of RAF Signals, BBC, ITN, the press and onlookers, together with the films and pictures that had been taken, we began a thorough analysis. Tony James (who did a great job in engineering the installation of the Orpheus engine into K7 at Norris Brothers, Haywards Heath) played a major part in this analysis.

Initial Explanations

The aerodynamics of a hydroplane are determined by its speed, its centre of gravity, centre of buoyancy, the ballast, its planing angles, the thrust of the engine and aerodynamic lift. So long as these remain within the designer's defined limits, the craft should remain in a stable position.

The weight of K7 and the thrust of its jet engine exerted a moment about the centre of gravity, pushing the nose down; onward airflow created upward pressure below the hull and suction above due to aerofoil-type behaviour, pushing the nose up. Wind-tunnel tests were carried out for the Norris brothers and the results are shown in diagram (a) opposite. As can be seen, at any given speed, the angle of incidence to the datum (i.e. water surface) must not exceed a critical upper value called the upper pitching incidence limit or 'safe operating envelope' – otherwise the boat will flip backwards. The initial design used a Beryl jet engine, and its safe operating envelope is seen to be 8 degrees at 250 mph. The more powerful Orpheus-engined boat, if travelling at 300 mph, had a smaller safe operating envelope of 6 degrees (Point 'A' on diagram [b]). Full fuel load and jet thrust

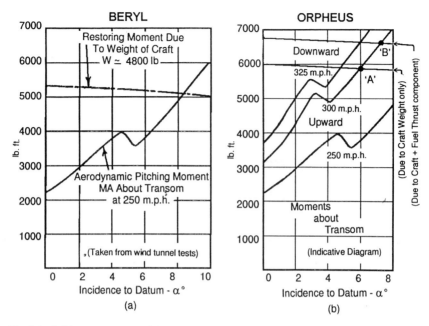

Fig. (a): pitching moment as a function of pitch angle intersecting the restoring moment near 8 degrees from wind-tunnel tests of an eighth-scale model of *Bluebird* conducted at Imperial College in February 1957 (Courtesy of *The Engineer*). Fig. (b): the general form of a family of speed curves estimated for the heavier Orpheus-engined K7 *(Courtesy of Philip Briggs)*

transiently increase the angle (Point 'B'). Calculations indicated that the upper safe speed of the Orpheus version was 350 mph, taking into account limited adverse water conditions.

Campbell did not wait for the wash from the first run, including that from the water brake, to subside before the return run and, by thus aggravating the pitch angle, this was a major cause of the accident. He did not refuel after his first run and this lowered the safety limit from 'B' towards 'A'. When he realised he was in trouble, he throttled back (see page 185, "I'm having to draw back"), so that the nose-down moment of K7 was reduced and the instantaneous safety angle exceeded. A more extreme scenario would have occurred if he had run out of fuel but, after so many years, it is pointless to speculate on why only a small amount of fuel was found in the tank of *Bluebird.*

Other theories have been proposed, including the striking of debris and aerodynamic instability due to previous birdstrikes. Neither is now thought to have been significant in this particular crash – but Ken Norris believes he can now explain more precisely what caused the accident.

The Nightmare Ride

The diagram on the facing page shows the speed curve of *Bluebird* on its final journey, together with the actual words of Donald Campbell. But what did go wrong? Are the accepted explanations correct? Ken Norris thinks not and he takes a mental ride to find out. Ken's words are shown in plain text, like this, comments are in *italic text* and Donald's words are in **bold text**:

I shut my eyes and turn off the mental pictures in my brain to black. I refuse to see anything but black, then switch on with my imagination in overdrive.

I'm Donald Campbell. I'm a pilot – disciplined and very safety conscious. All pre-run checks done. I'm taxiing in my old friend K7 to make my first run for a record over 300 mph. My concentration is absolute on this purpose.

Slow, steady turn to line up on course for my target.

Check radio reports – *'Slight swell – conditions look reasonably good – it's worth a try Skipper' comes the report from station Able (Leo Villa).*

Engine r.p.m., temperatures and pressures. Water brake off.

Here we go. Fire rockets. Radio silence.

Throttle up gently. K7's nose pitches down – a bit more throttle – K7 speeds up and nose starts to lift slowly.

More throttle – 70 mph – apply water brake sharply then turn left just as sharply and up comes the back of K7 and we're through the water drag hump and onto the planes – water brake off and steering straight ahead.

Acceleration is tremendous. Concentration on driving is paramount. Mental count – 1 and 2 and 3 and 4 and 5 and 6 and 7 and 8 and 9 and 10 seconds to 150 mph. Trim perfect – steady as a rock.

50 seconds and I'm accelerating past the first kilometre mark. 1 and 2 and 3 and 4 and 5 and 6 seconds and we're past the exit kilometre marker.

Throttle back gently. Speed dropping to 200 mph – seat belt keeping me upright against G-force.

Water brake on – a ton of extra drag – more 'G' pull on my seat belt. Down to 80 mph – water brake off. Passing Peel Island – 60 mph.

Throttle sufficient to keep 'on the step' and I'm passing the fuel boat.

Full House, Full House – a great run, no tramping. Call base – speed +47 *(i.e. 297 mph through the kilometre; 'tramping' = side-to-side rolling of the boat)*

Think, think – do I make a return run without refuelling? After all, I did it on Christmas Day and the run was OK. Think of it – in two to three minutes all the frustration could be over and we would have a record.

Decision made.

Stand by all stations, I'm making my return run.

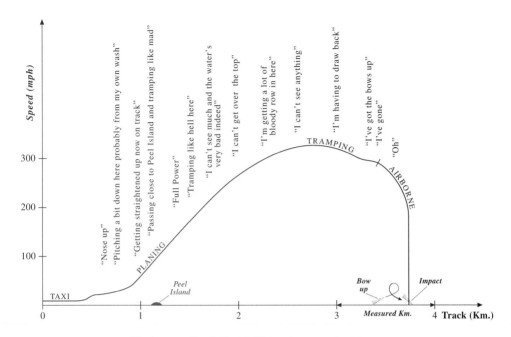

Final run profile of *Bluebird* K7 on January 4th 1967

Four-minute turnaround and I'm still on the planes taxiing at 50 mph and I've got a much longer run up to the kilometre. Fuel should be OK. Check instruments – throttle up – nose up.

70 mph: **Pitching a bit down here, probably from my own wash . . . Straightening up now in my track** . . . More throttle.

100 mph: **Passing close to Peel Island . . . Tramping like mad . . . Full power . . . Tramping like hell here . . .**

200 mph: **I can't see much and the water's very bad indeed** . . . *(Wash from water brake on first run getting to be like concrete with rocks spread on it. Water is 815 times the density of air. Eyeball oscillations have set in.)*

270 mph: **I can't get over the top . . .**" *(Can't get through the kilometre)*

300 mph: **I'm getting a lot of bloody row in here** . . . *(Mostly water noise due to tramping oscillations and lake surface conditions from first run, particularly water brake wash.)*

Over 320 mph: **I can't see anything . . . I'm having to draw back . . .**" *(Spray from tramping. Eyeball oscillations affecting vision.)*

290 mph: **I've got the bows up** . . . *(Less nose-down pitch from engine thrust – but K7 should not be at her safety incidence limit of 6 degrees)*

I've gone . . . Oh . . .

What *couldn't* happen, *did* happen

What was the significant difference between the first and second runs, apart from lake conditions? Ken Norris claims that it was *tramping*: a side-to-side rolling motion familiar to Donald's team and thought of as a nuisance, particularly on a return run, but of no real danger. But tramping on a *triangle*? When planing, the stability triangle of K7 – see opposite page – is an isosceles triangle: the base is formed by the two forward planing points and its apex is at the transom. Tramping on this triangle takes place about the two askew axes joining front to rear from each side. This causes a rise in pitching incidence, fluctuating from side to side as rolling takes place. The rolling and pitching angles are coupled, resulting in 'roll-induced pitch'. This would not have happened if K7 had been a four-pointer with a stability *rectangle*.

On *Bluebird*'s final run Donald complained of tramping and Keith Harrison (page 139) said "I saw her starboard sponson lift about 12 inches". If a sponson lifts in this type of design, the nose will lift with it. The tramping was caused by the sponsons hitting the swell and the waves on the surface of the lake. Tramping of any magnitude will, therefore, reduce the safety margin.

Calculations

The pitching incidence safety limit for the 'Orpheus' *Bluebird* at 300 mph was 6 degrees. Three significant factors contributed to the nose going up. In order of importance, these were:

Due to lift from increased air pressure caused by speed in excess of 300 mph: 1 degree (lift increases with square of speed)

Due to observed swell on lake: 1.5 degrees (five inches front to back, with a swell waveform of two boat lengths)

Due to tramping: 2.7 degrees (1ft over 16ft = 3.6 degrees at sponson; 1.8 degrees at centre line of hull; average 2.7 degrees)

The sum of these is 5.2 degrees, so the safety margin is now just 0.8 degrees and lift-off is imminent. The engine is pushing the nose down and the airflow is pushing it up. As the engine power reduced, so did the moment keeping the nose down; the imbalanced airflow then caused the nose to rise out of the water. The two main reductions in nose-down pitch were due to:

Half-full fuel tank: 224 lbs x 10.6 ft = 2390 lbs ft

Reduction in thrust, engine at half throttle: 2500 lbs x 0.5 ft from centre of gravity = 1250 lbs ft

Even so, the now-recommended application of the hydraulically-operated water brake would have saved the day.

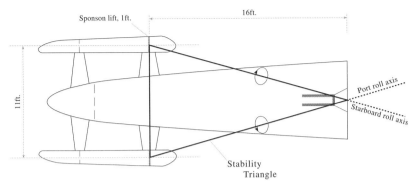

The Stability Triangle for K7

If the water brake had been applied before lift-off:

Gain in nose-down pitch if water brake used at 290 mph = 6994 lbs ft

Or, if used at top speed of 329 mph = 9000 lbs ft

So the loss of nose-down pitch due to thrust reduction could easily have been countered. Intriguingly, in the *Bluebird* wreck, the water brake was in the 'down' position. Campbell had clearly tried to use it, but too late – he was already airborne.

Conclusions

Ken Norris concluded his analysis with these words: "When Donald met disaster in K7 on 4 January 1967 he was 2 to 3 seconds away from gaining a new record at around 320 mph. His courage and determination to achieve this objective failed due to water surface conditions coupled with inherent stability limitations of K7 itself. It is ironic that the water brake (fitted to save him from overshooting the lake onto the shore) which created havoc with water conditions on his first run, could have been his life saver had he used it before he throttled back on the fatal run.

"Donald has left a vast legacy of knowledge which benefits dramatically all those who wish to challenge nature and break speed records. We must thank him sincerely and make good use of this knowledge. One thing is for certain: Donald was not on a mission to end his life. He was too full of life. He gave colour to life. He was after a record and he is missed by all of us."

*   *   *   *

Note: examination of the wreck in the summer of 2001 revealed that the front engine mounting had broken. If this occurred before the crash, instability might have ensued – but Campbell's words gave no hint of any sudden structural failure and it may equally well have snapped as *Bluebird* cartwheeled down the lake. Ken Norris stands by his original analysis, however.

20

The K7 Club

ON a warm autumn day in the year 2000, beside a peaceful lake that was disturbed by an occasional high-powered speedboat, Graham Beech interviewed Ray Hewartson during Windermere Records Week. Ray worked as a mechanic on the Windermere Motor Boat Racing Club boats almost 40 years ago and he knew Donald Campbell and many of the other big names of the British racing boat scene. He has been involved with powerboating for a magnificent 63 years and was chairman of the Windermere Water Speeds Record Club (WWSRC) for 2000/2001.

*   *   *   *

Just what is "K7"? Well, on the starboard sponson of Donald Campbell's *Bluebird* there was a design with a "sideways eight" – the mathematical sign for infinity – above "K7". The K simply indicates the Lloyds "unlimited" group, which has included:

K1: *Miss England III*, designed by Fred Cooper

K2: *Miss Britain III*, designed by Hubert Scott-Paine

K3: Malcolm Campbell's first *Bluebird*

K4: Malcolm Campbell's 1939 *Bluebird*, built by Saunders Roe

K5: *White Hawk*, driven by Frank Hanning-Lee

K6: John Cobb's *Crusader*, powered by a De Havilland Ghost turbojet

K7: The final version of *Bluebird* designed by the Norris brothers

K8: Tony Fahey's *British Pursuit*

The K7 Club is a tribute to Donald Campbell's contributions to British water speed record attempts, though the organisation has links with the Rocket Club associated with the name of Sir

Malcolm Campbell. If Malcolm "gave you a rocket" for some misdemeanour, you were well on your way to membership of this merry band of typically British enthusiasts. Members included Leo Villa, Maurice Parfitt, Ray Hewartson, Bill Coley and Greville Howard, all of whom transferred from the Rocket Club to K7 in 1955 with the aim of maintaining *Bluebird* expertise and support while Donald Campbell was in the USA, attempting to break more records. Early K7 members included Norman Buckley (Chairman and record attempt timekeeper), Keith Harrison (Secretary/treasurer), Ken Norris (co-designer of the K7 *Bluebird*), Andrew Brown, Sir William Butlin (of holiday camp fame), Cdr. Errol Bruce, Capt. John Coote, Ken Reakes, Lord Wakefield (Castrol Oil Company), Geoffrey Hallawell (photographer) and Harry Griffin – the journalist responsible for breaking the news of Donald Campbell's fatal crash in 1967, and who was present at every one of his record attempts in England.

The club first met at the Glenridding Hotel on the shores of Ullswater, then home to *Bluebird*. In July 1955, they left for Coniston and, just ten years later, a new phase began, still under the chairmanship of Norman Buckley. Norman owned the Low Wood Hotel and, significantly, a stretch of the Windermere foreshore. He was passionately keen on powerboat racing and, as a member of the Windermere Motorboat Racing Club (WMBRC), began breaking various records. Norman struck up a friendship with William Lyons and Lofty England, both of Jaguar Cars, and this led to the incorporation of a 3.8 litre Jaguar engine in the highly successful *Miss Windermere* series of boats. Norman Buckley's own record attempts required official timing and so, to make better use of his timekeepers, he invited other enthusiasts to join him in a whole week of record attempts: Windermere Records Week. A new organisation was formed, the Windermere Water Speeds Record Club (WWSRC).

The K7 Club is still active, with around 150 members, many of whom are also in the WWSRC. It is a "by invitation" organisation and prospective members need to demonstrate at least five years involvement in record attempts. The current committee includes Ken Norris (President); Robin Brown (Chairman); Richard Solomon (Secretary); Dennis Heaton – one-time hydroplane racer; and Ron Beatty, a Jaguar engines development engineer.

Nowadays, the club has a wider brief than when it was first

Secretary of the K7 Club, Richard Solomon (left) and Robin Brown, Chairman, at the
Campbell Memorial on January 4th, 2001 *(North-West Evening Mail)*

formed, being concerned with assisting and promoting all
manner of British record attempts on land, sea and air. The club
also provides a social dimension to the world of record attempts,
with an annual meeting at the WMBRC. Their lasting achievement is the Campbell Memorial, which stands in the centre of
the village of Coniston. Built in the form of a George Cross by
George Usher, a local stonemason, using stone from Coniston
Old Man, it was unveiled in 1969 by Dorothy, Lady Campbell.
Each year since 1985, it has been the focus of a short memorial
service where, at 11 am on January 4th, the K7 Prayer has been
read:

> We laughed with you, we cheered with you
> We urged you on, we cried for you
> We prayed for you, we mourned for you
> We always will.
> 30 years have passed, but we still dwell on the time
> When we shared your glory
> And now dear Donald in our hearts we keep you close
> And may the Lord hold you in the palm of his hand
> In our beautiful Coniston Water.

21

Living the Legend

The Campbell legend has inspired books, paintings, memorabilia, and exhibits. Here is a selection that should be of interest to those who would like to delve deeper:

The Lakeland Motor Museum

Situated within Holker Hall and Gardens in South Lakeland and signposted from Junction 36 on the M6 via the A590, 'Motoring Memories' at the Lakeland Motor Museum provides a nostalgic experience and a reminder of transport bygones from pioneering motoring of the early 1900s, through to the 1950s with a particular emphasis on Sir Malcolm and Donald Campbell, with the unique 'Campbell Legend Bluebird Exhibition'. Highlights include full-size replicas of the 1935 *Bluebird* car and of *Bluebird* K7, used, respectively, in the BBC films, 'Speed Kings' starring Robert Hardy and 'Across the Lake', in which Anthony Hopkins portrayed Donald Campbell.

The exhibits are complemented by a rare example of the *Jet-Star* speed boat used as a service craft during record attempts and a 1936 Bentley 4¼ litre, once owned and driven by Donald Campbell, hence the colour, Bluebird blue. Scale models, photographs of the cars and boats used in the record attempts, a replica of Donald's mascot, 'Mr Whoppit', and continuous video commemorate these childhood heroes. The shop has a good range of books and models. Open April to October inclusive, Sunday to Friday (closed Saturdays) 10.30am to 4.45pm. Admission includes the award-winning gardens and the opportunity to visit Holker Hall, the residence of Lord and Lady Cavenish. Web site: http://www.instinct-training.co.uk/ti/sl/holkmus.htm

The Ruskin Museum

This museum is in Yewdale Road, Coniston. Displays illustrate Coniston's history from the Stone Age to the jet era and reflect John Ruskin's own enthusiasm and philosophy. Ruskin was a Victorian social reformer and early ecologist who, with Donald Campbell, shared the belief that "nowt caps Coniston". The people of Coniston cherish their memory, and have made sure that the museum contains a suitable commemoration (with kind assistance from the Lakeland Motor Museum at Holker Hall) of Sir Malcolm and Donald Campbell, and the succession of boats called *Bluebird* which once sped over Coniston Water. Photographs, press cuttings, personal memorabilia, film footage and a crumpled section of sponson tell the story of the Campbells' attempts to be the fastest men on water, anywhere.

The museum was extended and re-developed in 1998/99 thanks to an £850,000 project funded in part by the Heritage Lottery Fund. It is open from Easter/1st April (whichever is earlier) to mid-November 10.00 am to 5.30 pm daily; rest of the year, Wednesday to Sunday inclusive, 10.30 am to 3.30 pm. Closed 24th-26th December and 1st January. Tel: 015394 41164; fax: 015394 41132. Web site: www.coniston.org.uk.

Filching Manor

This private collection is housed in a medieval manor in Polegate, Sussex and visits can be arranged for groups by appointment only – phone 01323-487838 for further details. In addition to a collection of over 100 cars the present owner, Paul Foulkes-Halbard, has created a "Campbell Memorial Hall" featuring a replica of the K7 *Bluebird*, and various artefacts from personal possessions to complete engines. Sir Malcolm Campbell's K3 *Bluebird* has been restored and is on display, as are boats that belonged to Gina Campbell. Paul had claimed to own the wreck of *Bluebird* K7 – see final pages of Chapter 18.

The Bluebird Café

Standing on the shore of Coniston Water, the building dates from 1860, when it was a mess hut for the crew of the original steam yacht *Gondola*. It became a café in the 1960s and was in use during the 1966/67 record attempts. Phil and Judith Dixon have been the proprietors since 1982. A range of postcards and other memorabilia is available. Web site: www.thebluebirdcafe.com

Memorabilia

For archive posters and photographs, try Schofield's Speed Auction, P.O. Box 48, New Braintree MA, 01531 USA. Tel: (508) 867-3545. Email: schofieldauction@mindspring.com.

Paintings

Prints from original paintings are available from:

Moving Images: 1 Severn Side, Stourport-on-Severn, Worcestershire DY13 9EN. Tel: 01299 822441. Fax: 01299 823225. E-mail: jon@advertisingmatters.com.

Arthur Benjamins: "Blue Bird Publications", 162 Swievelands Road, Biggin Hill, Kent, TN16 3QX. Tel: 01959 574414. Fax: 01959 571077. E-mail: bbirdpubl@aol.com.

Models

Scale models of *Bluebird* (1955, 1964 and 1967 versions) are available from Replicast Record Models. Web site: www.merseyworld.com/replicast. Tel: 01704-542233.

One of the Replicast range of scale models.

Books

Most of the following books are out of print but second-hand copies can usually be obtained – try www.bibliofind.com or the Hydroplane and Raceboat Museum, 1605 South 93rd Street Building E-D, Seattle, Washington 98108. Tel: (206) 764-9453.

With Campbell at Coniston, First Edition, Arthur Knowles (William Kimber, 1967)

Bluebirds – the Story of the Campbell Dynasty, Gina Campbell and Michael Meech (Sidgwick and Jackson, 1988)

Donald Campbell CBE, Arthur Knowles and Dorothy, Lady Campbell (George Allen and Unwin, 1969)

The Fastest Men on Earth: 100 years of the Land Speed Record, P.J.R. Holthusen and Art Arfons, (Sutton Publishing, 1996)

The Fastest Men on Earth: the men and cars that smashed the World Land Speed Record, Paul Clifton (Herbert and Jackson, 1966)

Into the Water Barrier, Donald Campbell (Odhams, 1955)

Bluebird and The Dead Lake, John Pearson (Collins, 1965)

The Record Breakers: Sir Malcolm and Donald Campbell: Land and Water Speed Kings of the 20th Century, Leo Villa and Tony Gray (Hamlyn Publishing Group Ltd, 1969)

The World Water Speed Record, Leo Villa and Kevin Desmond (B.T. Batsford Ltd, 1976)

The John Cobb Story, S.C.H. Davis (Foulis, 1952)

Kaye Don – the Man, James Wentworth Day (Hutchinson, 1934)

Sir Henry Segrave, Cyril Posthumus (James, 1968)

Internet

Enthusiasts and 'anoraks' are well catered for on the web:

A well-established Campbell tribute website, run by Dean Cox, is **Across The Lake** – packed with information and with links to many other sites: www.acrossthelake.com

Andy Griffin runs the **Speed Record Discussion Group**, mainly concerned with Donald Campbell. To join the group, go to: http://groups.yahoo.com/group/Speedrecordgroup This brings up the main page; on the top right-hand side is "Join this group"– click on here and follow the instructions.

For the official **Bluebird Project** site, with details of how the *Bluebird* wreck was recovered, go to: www.bluebirdproject.com

One of the most comprehensive **hydroplane websites** is www.lesliefield.com. It includes an **archive photo gallery:** www.lesliefield.com/galleries/donald_campbell_and_bluebird.htm

Also very worthwhile is the **Seattle Hydroplane and Raceboat Museum**: www.thunderboats.org – from where you can download a video clip of the final moments of the 1967 *Bluebird* run. **Note:** the same clip can be downloaded from the publisher's UK web site at www.sigmapress.co.uk.

A useful **general site** for current boats is: www.hydroplane.net

22 _____

Beyond the next barrier?

THE world water-speed record has been broken three times
since Donald Campbell's triumph on Lake Dumbleyung in
1964. It has stood at 317.60 mph since Australia's Ken Warby
broke the 300 mph barrier in his *Spirit of Australia* in October
1978. Ken Warby and England's Nigel Macknight, have
announced plans to raise the record still higher. Another potential contender is Australia's *Southern Cross Water Shuttle*,
though little is known about this. Perhaps the rivalry between
England and Australia will be sufficient to fire the public's
imagination – is 350 mph, or even 400 mph the next barrier?

Spirit of Australia

After more than 20 years, Ken Warby is preparing to break his
own record. Ken's revamped boat is powered by a 9,000 h.p.
Westinghouse turbojet, but the boat itself is very similar to his

Ken Warby's *Spirit of Australia*

1978 record-breaker. Construction was completed in December 1999 and a record attempt is planned with Ken or his son Dave as driver. Commercial sponsors are being sought (October 2001).

Further details can be obtained from Ken's web site:

www.kenwarby.com

– where you can leave your comments, questions and offers of sponsorship!

Quicksilver

The British contender is the *Quicksilver* project, led by Nigel Macknight. The chief designer is Ken Norris, co-designer of the K7 *Bluebird*. The powerplant is a single Rolls-Royce Spey 101 turbofan engine – two of which have been obtained by purchasing an ex-RAF Buccaneer strike aircraft. A third engine has also been acquired as a backup.

Quicksilver has been designed as a four-pointer, a unique configuration in world water speed record history. Its structure is based on a combination of high-tensile steel tubing manufactured by Accles & Pollock and honeycomb sandwich panels by Hexcel Composites. Accles & Pollock and Hexcel played key roles in the construction of Donald Campbell's *Bluebird* boat and car respectively.

Water tank tests of models have been completed and, by October 2001, both hull fabrication and engine testing were reported to be progressing satisfactorily. No photographs are yet available of the final craft, though an artist's impression has been produced, as shown on the following page. This is available in full colour from Moving Images – see the final page of this book.

There is also a web site:
www.quicksilver-wsr.co.uk

Design and operation

Ken Norris, *Quicksilver*'s chief designer, concludes:

❏ Take steps to remove as much kite area (see page 36) as possible and revert to a four-pointer canard design with tail plane to improve aerodynamic stability/operational pitching envelope. This causes the stability triangle (page 187) to be reversed and to be made much longer than in *Bluebird* K7.

❏ Beware the deadly swell – it has no mercy. Operate only in calm conditions with no swell. Swell can, if large enough, absorb all of the pitching safety limit in one go.

❏ Allow water to calm down after first run, because of too much water brake disturbance.

❏ Fit active water trimmers: the weight carried on the water to be at least the full weight of the machine, allowing for water drag/air drag being within record limits.

❏ Beware of assymetry due to structural damage (e.g. bird strikes and debris in the lake) as these could aggravate or instigate tramping.

❏ Beware the wicked water brake. Operational procedure is to use it before throttling down.

Quicksilver, by John Pittaway *(by permission of Moving Images)*

American Challenge WSR

Since the previous reprint of this book, a third contender has entered the race to become the fastest man on water. On 3rd August 2001, Russ Wicks, holder of the speed record for propeller-driven boats (see page 23), announced his intention to try to break the World Water Speed Record. The project is based in the Seattle area and backed by a consortium of aerospace engineers and technology companies.

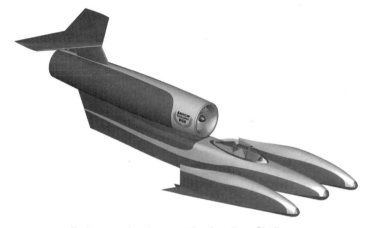

Early promotional concept for *American Challenge*

Though the *Spirit of Australia* and *Quicksilver* teams are at a more advanced stage, Russ Wicks is an experienced hydroplane driver and *American Challenge* could well be a serious rival. Design work has commenced on a hydroplane with two forward planing points and test runs are planned for 2003 on Lake Washington – a famous location in water speed record history.

The entry of an American challenger at this stage is reminiscent of the events that spurred Donald Campbell to make his bid to take *Bluebird* past 300 mph. When asked, in October 1966, why he was doing it, his reply was "Because the Americans are spending millions of dollars trying to get this record from Britain. The way to beat them is to bump it out of their reach before they even get started." Nigel Macknight and Ken Warby doubtless share this sentiment.

Further details of *American Challenge WSR* will be posted on Russ Wicks' web site: www.russwicks.com